• Dave Adolph • Gale Adolph • Marvena Agnew • Robert Aguilera • Alan Ahlers • Mark Ahlers • Scott Ahlers • Michael Ahrens • Glen Ahrenstorff •
xander • Theresa Alexander • Kirby Andersen • Brian Anderson • Christopher Anderson • Debra Anderson • Donna Anderson • Jerry Anderson • John
Arends • Benjamin Asrat • Christi Audiss • Danny Ault • Ray Austin • Judy Babb • Brenda Baerenwald • Richard Bakken • Barbara Bakker • Herman
meister • Eunice Baumgard • Joe Baumgartner • Kevin Baumgartner • Curtis Becker • Dan Becker • Randy Becker • James Beckman • Jeff Beckman •
Bents • Wayne Bents • Harvey Berg • Penny Berg • Richard Bergen • Dennis Berger • Joy Berger • Mike Berger • Jean Bianchi • Kathy Bickett • LeAnn
Edward Bohn • Sharon Bohnenkamp • Bill Bohning • Joni Bohning • Bruce Bohning • Abby Boltjes • Bruce Boltjes • Jane Boneschans • Gary Borgers
Kenneth Brandt • Jonathan Brassfield • Andy Braun • Paul Braun • Roseanne Breuer • Michael Brew • Bryan Brink • Jeff Brink • Linda Broich • Mark
Bruse • Pam Bruse • Melissa Brust • Angie Bryngelson • Brad Bryngelson • Janice Bryngelson • Gerald Brynjulson • Cathy Bucciarelli • Elvera Bucher
ister • Teri Burmeister • Duane Burmeister • Robert Burmeister • Scott Burns • Theresa Burrgraff • Steve Bury • Chris Buss • Jeff Buysman • Randy
• Randall Childers • Kathryn Christians • Darwin Christians • Lester Clark • Gaylcen Clauson • Buddy Claypool • Sonja Claypool • Pam Colby • Terry
Cox • John Cramer • Charles Crews • Blair Crockett • Rick Cross • Judy Cummings • Pam Cuperus • George Curtis • Tai Dahn • Matt Damon • David
ve Denbow • Dan Dettman • Debbie Deutsch • Debbie Deutsch • Donn Develder • Clifford Devins • Esther DeWeerd • Craig Dice • Dan Diekmann
ade Domres • Luann Dooley • Carolyn Doornewcerd • Judy Doppenberg • Matt Dorn • Mary Douglas • Stan Drietz • Robert Dronen • Sheryl DuBois
• Ken Eichmann • Kirk Eidhammer • Robert Eilders • Monte Einck • Sharon Ella • Edward Ellison • Cindy Else • Jessica Elsing • Kevin Elsing • Robert
son • Daniel Erickson • Lee Erpelding • Douglas Erwin • Kevin Evans • Wayne Evans • Mark Evensen • Deborah Everett • Keith Evers • Shane Evers
er • David Ferdinand • Tracy Fergeson • Lois Ferguson • Jill Fernette • Nancy Fields • Ray Fields • Scott Finnesgard • Keith Fisher • LaDonn Fisher
ndon Freking • Debra Frerichs • Patti Frey • Richard Frey • Al Fricke • Rebecca Frisch • Susan Fritel • Adam Fritz • John Fritz • Dean Fritz • Les
ujan • Travis Funk • Darlene Furrer • Shelley Gaddes • Shelly Gades • Michael Galagan • Shane Gallcs • Bob Gantzer • Richard Garmer • Zeke Gaska
er • Tracy Giugler • Jim Gleitz • Jesse Gloe • Dale Glover • Vicki Goblirsch • Vicky Goblirsch • Dennis Goebel • Judy Goedderz • Michael Goettig •
aine Graphenteen • Robin Grave • Joyce Gravon • Christine Greeley • Dale Greeley • Lisa Green • Michelle Greve • Randal Griffith • Timothy Griffith
d Groenwold • David Groff • Ardes Gronewold • Bobbie Gronewold • Dan Gronewold • Randy Gronewold • Duane Gruis • Bonnie Grunewald • Nida
Habeck • Herman Habeck • Melissa Habeck • Rochelle Habeck • Daniel Haberman • Doreen Haberman • Lois Haberman • Mary Haberman • Teresa
• Todd Hallsrom • Mike Hamman • David Hand • David Hansbauer • Harry Hansbauer • Bruce Hansberger • Dale Hanson • Mary Hanson • Virgil
Harvey • Terryl Harvey • Edward Hassing • Donald Haubrich • Chris Hawkinson • Dan Hawkinson • Sheila Hawkinson • Tim Hawkinson • Lonnie
eiden • Jason Heimstra • Curt Heinrichs • Lisa Heinrichs • Ron Heinrichs • Steve Heinrichs • Tammy Heintz • Jeff Heitkamp • Terry Helget • Harlan
ori Henning • Luke Henning • Radley Hennings • Jessie Hernandez • Charles Herreid • Susan Hickman • Jason Hienstra • Gene Hieronimus • Gary
Hinrichs • Lien Hinrichs • James Hintgen • Jenny Hintgen • Arlene Hinz • Judi Hinz • Dennis Hitzemann • James Hitzemann • Jim Hodgkin • Ranzie
ohensee • Cassandra Hohensee • Hope Holland • Becky Holmes • Dale Holmes • Michael Holmes • Peter Honerman • Paul Honken • Grover Hooper
• Wayne Huls • Dave Hurlburt • Delbert Hurley • Robin Hval • Wayne Irby • Janet Isder • Brian Iverson • Donald Jacobs • Elaine Jacobs • Lois Jacobs
Jeff Jenkins • Karen Jenkins • Craid Jepperson • Roger Jesson • Jessica Joens • Joy Joens • Kim Johanning • Darwin Johansen • Amber Johlfs • Larry
erald Johnson • Kim Johnson • Lonnie Johnson • Marty Johnson • Steve Johnson • Carol Johnson • Craig Johnson • Donna Johnson • Michelle Johnson
lly Julius • Karen Jungjohan • Lori Junker • Randy Junker • Dale Jurgensen • David Jurgensen • Terry Jurrens • John Jr Juza • Daniel Kahl • Roland
King • Randy King • Paula Kingery • Doreen Kjelden • Ted Klein • Julie Kleinvachter • Barry Kleinwolterink • Gary Klenken • Gary Kleve • Walter
Mike Knorr • Dennis Koehler • Twyla Kok • Audrey Kolander • Donna Koning • Del Koopman • Betty Koopmeiners • Anne Koppy • Mary Kor • Tim
uer • Sharon Krieger-Maltas • Tom Krogman • Janelle Krogman • Mary Krueger • Jason Kruger • Kyle Kruger • Mellissa Kruger • Al Kruse • Robert
Donald Kunzweiler • Dawn Kuperus • Terry Kusserow • Catherine Lade • Steve Lade • Jeff Lair • Gene Lais • Thad Lambert • Scott Lambert • Jim
Larsen • Anita Larson • Eugene Larson • Keith Larson • Sylvia Larson • Alan Laue • Janet Laufmann • Bob Lauro • David Lawrence • Chris Lawson
y Lemke • Tom Lemke • Thomas Lenarz • Mitchell Leopold • Dick Lesch • Jack Leslie • Jim Lesnar • Ben Lewis • Richard Liapis • Glen Libra • Craig
an • Guy Longbrake • Gary Lonneman • Bruce Lonneman • Chad Loosbrock • Michael Loosbrock • Kris Loosbrock • Joe Lopez • Teresa Lottman
z • Barbara Lund • Janet Lutson • Dawn Lykken • Lester Lyon • Marty Lyons • Darrel Maher • Dennis Malcolm • Jewell Malenke • Donnie Malmgren
• Loren Marsh • Ryan Marsh • Linda Martens • Dale Martin • Martha Mastbergen • Pam Mastbergen • Rodney Mastbergen • Alice Mathias • Benjamin
ay • Hans May • Karla May • Sam Mayo • David McCall • Greg McCarthy • Greg McCarty • Julie McCarvel • Julia McClintick • Bill McClintock • Sue
erkel • Amy Merrill • Jeff Metz • Clint Meyer • Lee Meyer • Myron Meyer • Joan Meyeraan • Roger Meyeraan • Jay Milbrandt • Kim Milbrandt • Sarah
r • Dan Moet • Yvonne Moknos • Ernie Monsees • Terri Montanez • Doyle Moore • Larry Morfitt • Fred Moriston • Gary Morris • Mark Morrison •
Nelson • John Nelson • Scott Nelson • Susan Nelson • Travis Nelson • Lori Nelson • Mervin Nelson • Peggy Nelson • Kevin Nesdahl • Lawrence Ness
Noram • Paul Nordell • Melvin Norem • Robert Norris • Richard Nunes • Mark Nyberg • Randy Nygaard • John O'Brien • Michael O'Donnell • Jennifer
lsem • Ole Olson • Penny Olthoff • Donald Oltmans • Kraig Onken • Bruce Orke • Kandy Osterkamp • Ann Osterkamp • Shawn Otterson • Orville
aulsen • Herman Jr Paulsen • Darrold Peck • Darren Peck • Michael E Pederson • Reid Pederson • Erik Pederson • Rao Pemmeraju • Jay Person • Rich
erson • Nels Peterson • Toni Peterson • Wayne Peterson • Beverly Peterson • Chris Pfeil • Tom Pfeil • Curt Pheifer • Audra Phillips • Gary Pickering
chard • Dean Pritchett • Jan Puck • Deb Pueppke • Scott Pueppke • Roxanne Putnam • Jackie Quarnstrom • Doug Quiring • Janice Quiring • Sharon
g • Harvey Ray • Cynthia Rector • Panda Reimers • Daniel Reineke • David Reincke • Paul Reisdorfer • Rose Reisdorfer • Ken Reiter • Harold
• Robert Renken • Robert Renken • Kelly Reum • Glen Reuter • Lois Reuter • David Rick • Jay Riddle • Susan Riddle • Linda Rients • David
rbanck • Dick Rohwedder • Roger Roland • Beverly Roland • Terry Ronk • Timothy Roos • Dale Ross • Lindia Roth • Gerus Rubingh • Jessie
Ryle • Scott Sagmoe • Brian Salter • Rich Salvaggio • Todd Samp • Lorin Sandberg • Bonnie Sangl • Monty Sangl • Barbara Sankey • Dennis
charlepp • Jim Scheepstra • Randy Scheepstra • Douglas Scheerhorn • Dave Scheffler • Barb Schei • Paula Scheidt • Thad Schetnan • Gary
t Schreur • Ritchie Schriever • Cindy Schroeder • Josh Schroeder • Ryan Schroeder • Tami Schroeder • Todd Schroeder • Torey Schroeder •
Peggy Schuur • Todd Schuur • Darrell Schuur • Roger Schwab • Dawn Schwebach • David Schweigert • Ron Schweigert • Louis Schweigert •
Dave Shepherd • Arthur Sherer • Dan Shipley • Tom Shore • Bill Shoup • Jim Shows • Xay Sidadorane • Robert Sieli • John Sietseman • Curt
• Jane Slocum • Mary Smeins • Harry Smith • Jim Smith • Joe Smith • Kelly Smith • Leonard Smith • Michealle Smith • Terry Smith • Gregory
essard • Steve Spessard • Lori Spidel • Sue Spillman • Verna Spottedwood • Janelle Sprague • Duane Staedtler • Paul Stam • Larry Stamer •
nberg • Danie Steinholt • Melissa Steinmetz • Ronald Sternke • Craig Stock • Paula Stock • Jeff Stokes • Steven Stokes • Tammy Stokes • Gene
lsma • Hue Tang • Melodie Tate • Jacqueline Taylor • Jarald Taylor • Jeffrey Taylor • John Taylor • Steve Taylor • Dan Teeslink • Jim Tengwall
nd Thorn • Al Thorson Monte Thue • Kenneth Thul • Karla Thuringer • Aiah Tieh • Jerald Tilton • Thomas Tilton • Kevin Timmemann • Bob
aby Toussaint • Robin Tow • Jeanene Townswick • Dung Tran • Phuong Tran • Thoi Tran • Linfs Triebenbach • David Tripp • Jeff Trunnell •
e Vacek • Ramon Valdivia • Marshall Van Domelen • Dan Van Ede • John A Van Ede • John C Van Ede • Kevin Van Malsen • Kevin Van Matsen
d VandeBrake • Steve VandeBrake • Nelma Vanden Bosch • Arlyn Vander Beek • Rose Vander Beek • Debra Vander Schaaf • Russell Vandergrift
• Courtney Voehl • Bill Vogelaar • Pete Vogelsang • Bradley Von Holdt • Julie Von Holdt • Tim Von Holdt • Betty Von Laar • Teresa VonHoltum
atricia Wallace • Mary Walter • Jeff Walters • Rod Waltjer • Kendall Ward • Mike Warner • Mark Weber • Jamie Weg • Tim Weg • Verlyn Weg
nifer Wibbens • Kolleen Wick • Teresa Widboom • Curt Wiencke • Tina Wiencke • Scott Wiertzema • Todd Wiertzema • Kim Wiertzema • Greg
itzel • Jan Witzel • Jim Witzel • Alice Wolf • Chris Wolf • Curt Wolfswinkel • Laurie Wolfswinkel • Shiree Wolfswinkel • Sandy Wolter • Merlin
ie Zabel • Rebecca Zabel • Gary Zandstra • Harry Zandt • Chuck Zemler • Kelly Zinnel • Marvin Zinnel • Gerald Zins • Jane Zins • Tom Zishka

A Twist of Innovation

Nothing in the world can take the place of persistence. Talent will not; nothing is more common than unsuccessful men with talent. Genius will not; unrewarded genius is almost a proverb. Education will not; the world is full of educated derelicts. Persistence and determination alone are omnipotent. The slogan "Press On" has solved and always will solve the problems of the human race.

—Calvin Coolidge

A Twist of Innovation

A History of Bedford Industries

The Hooge Boys,
I hope you enjoy
the Bedford story!

Jay A. Milbrandt

Bedford Industries, Inc. • Worthington, Minnesota • 2004

© 2004 by Bedford Industries, Inc.
1659 Rowe Avenue
Worthington, MN 56187
877-233-3673
All rights reserved.
Library of Congress Control Number: 2004113048
ISBN 0-9761839-0-0
Manufactured in the United States of America
10 9 8 7 6 5 4 3 2 1

On the cover:
The blind-stamped B, suggestive of Bedford Industries' first product—the twist tie—was the firm's first logo. See pages 66 and 145 for evolving versions of the logo.

Endsheets:
A cumulative (1966–June 2004) list of the employees of Bedford Industries, Inc.

Illustrations:
Most of the illustrations in this volume are from the collections and scrapbooks of Bedford Industries, Inc.

Newspaper and photographer credits appear in the captions for other photos, printed by permission.

The photo (originally in color) of the author on page 196 is the work of Rickers Photography Studio–Worthington.

Quotations:
Printed by permission of the *Worthington Daily Globe*, the *Arkansas Democrat Gazette*, *Minnesota Technology*, *Packaging Digest*, and *Tri-State Neighbor*.

Baking Industry, Consolidated Aluminum Corp. *(Reflections)*, *Craft and Needlework*, *Creative Products News*, and *Small Business Report* apparently are no longer in business.

Contents

To Robert and Patricia Ludlow
and the employees of Bedford Industries
who have contributed to its success

Preface

Not often does one have the opportunity to document a story such as that of *A Twist of Innovation*. More often one wishes to have done so in retrospect, after key figures are gone or important stories lost. The main premise of this work is the preservation of the history of Bedford Industries, Inc.

I believe that main goal has been accomplished, but I want to encourage another way to read this book, one broader than that of friends and employees of Bedford Industries, that of the general reader. *A Twist of Innovation* is a lively story of innovation and ingenuity revolving around a common household item—the twist tie. It is a testament to hard work and a group of people who wanted to improve on a product and service in an industry. As much as my grandfather, Robert Ludlow, attributes Bedford's success to luck, I challenge the reader to look for the many lessons to be learned from the example Bedford employees have set. This is a story from which anyone can learn.

While I have done my best to collect stories and facts, undoubtedly there are mistakes and missing pieces. For instance, while we have attempted a cumulative list of Bedford Industries employees (1966 to July 2004, see endpages), it is unlikely we have every name. Please contact Norma Cook or Kim Milbrandt at Bedford Industries if you know of others.

Many people have influenced the direction of this book. Numerous current and past employees and friends were willing to be interviewed, to proofread, help with research, and check on details. Ellen Green, my editor, improved the quality of the manuscript tenfold. She provided instruction in the art of writing and publishing, as well as support and encouragement.

Thanks also to the owners of some of the original twist-tie companies for their graciousness. The Bedford story would likely be much different if not for their work in the industry. See my essay, "A Twist of History," in the appendix, for the history of the twist tie and for the names of those who contributed.

The greatest thank-you goes to my grandparents, Bob and Pat Ludlow, to whom this book is dedicated. They are the reason I started writing, and I would not have finished without their continued help and dedication to the project. See Bob Ludlow's afterword for clarity on the underlying mission of Bedford Industries and the Ludlows.

At the end of this project, I look at Bedford in a different way than before. I cannot walk through the production floor without thinking about how the company started from scratch and about the work that went into it. I am in awe. And I hope every reader takes something from this story that will change his or her life.

–Jay Milbrandt

Prologue

Anyone claiming that a small midwestern town harbors the largest twist-tie manufacturer in the world might merit a skeptical smile. But in 1966, a husband and wife started a business in Worthington, Minnesota, that made it home to the company earning that title.

Who would think a business as large as Bedford Industries, making an item so familiar as the twist tie, could start in a small garage? Almost certainly, the people who started the ball rolling 40 years ago did not imagine a market extending from bakeries to coffee fields and surgical rooms. Much less could they have envisioned Bedford as one of the most technologically advanced packaging companies in the world!

Founder Robert (or Bob) Ludlow has said that the story of Bedford Industries is only 1 percent business-related—the other 99 percent is people. Bedford's success is due to those who put in long hours and late nights developing a product and creating an efficient process. Bedford's story is not one of highly trained engineers and business professionals but of motivated people with great imagination.

What makes Bedford different from other manufacturing firms? First, it is still in Worthington and under its original ownership. Now in transfer to a second generation, the company continues to grow. How has Bedford done this when so many others have failed or been bought out? The company fosters a certain chemistry—not a set of business and management principles, but something more aptly described as art. This art is exposed in the stories of current and past employees. What they know and have learned is the key to Bedford's success.

This book shares the stories of those responsible for Bedford's growth and prosperity. It seeks to put the pieces of the past together, to call forth the company's heart and soul, and to preserve that legacy as a tribute to its employees. It hopes to leave the reader with a sense of the art of innovation and of what the people of Bedford have to offer.

Bedford today

Edmund F. Ball, son of one of the founders of the Ball Corporation, once said, "Contrary to a popular misconception that corporations are cold, impersonal institutions possessing neither heart nor soul, each is an ever-changing mosaic composed of the composite characteristics of hundreds, maybe thousands, of individuals who have participated in the shaping of its image."

Ball's words aptly describe Bedford Industries. Bedford's heart and soul live in all of the people who have shaped the company over the years. Each employee has left a mark on the company, just as Bedford has left its mark on each of them.

This year, the company produced enough twist-tie ribbon to make three trips to the moon and back. Of the few remaining twist-tie manufacturers in the world, no other would make this claim. Bedford Industries helds the lead—and closely holds the history that has made this so.

Bedford is one of the most progressive innovators in packaging. The ideas and innovations making the company successful for almost 40 years are countless. Bedford has taken the simple twist tie and diversified it into more than 25 markets. The company sells well over 60 standard versions of the twist tie, not including its custom products. Mix that with close to 25 stock colors and the possibility of nine-color custom printing, and the Bedford product lineup expands exponentially.

Bedford's customers are as diverse as the use of its product. They include users in every state and in more than 60 countries—even Egypt, Guam, Indonesia, and Haiti. The customers are global conglomerates, nationwide suppliers, small farms, and family-owned stores.

Bedford's employees are diverse in location and interest. Most reside in Worthington, though many drive as much as an hour each way from South Dakota, Iowa, and other parts of Minnesota. Regional salespeople live and work across the United States—from Connecticut to California. After hours, the employees are involved in their communities. They serve as college professors and coaches, emergency personnel and church leaders, and on hospital boards and city councils.

Bedford is founded on community. The nonunionized company is still family-owned, with family members serving on its board of directors and as managers. The firm remains under original ownership and is in transfer to the second generation. The employees and their families often refer to themselves as "the Bedford family," a sign of the environment that is central to the organization.

The family feeling is visible in the loyalty of the employees—perhaps one of Bedford Industries' most notable achievements. One of the first employees, John Van Ede, said, "You'll never find a finer place to work. And that's why people stay." Every year, Bedford hosts a dinner to recognize its employees with 10,

20, 25, or 30 years of service. The gathering is large—Bedford now invites at least half its employees to the event. At least one-third of these have served 20 years or more.

Bedford Industries also holds a long tradition of bringing its extended family together. The company began its annual family get-together years ago; the first was a dinner in the basement of Michael's, a local steakhouse. The need for increasingly larger venues indicates Bedford's growth. At first, just 15 employees and their families attended. Now, the Bedford family picnics take place in venues that can handle 200 employees plus their families as well as invited retirees. In recent years the company has gathered in places such as the Hubert H. Humphrey Metrodome in Minneapolis for a Minnesota Twins baseball game, the Great Plains Zoo and Delbridge Museum of Natural History in Sioux Falls, South Dakota, and Arnolds Park near Okiboji, Iowa.

Bedford is still a hometown business. Worthington has shaped the company, and Bedford, one of its largest employers, has influenced the character of the town. With almost 200 on its payroll, Bedford is one of the local businesses most involved in the community. Like many small towns, Worthington's booming downtown of years gone by has fallen to large chain stores. City groups needing donations or funding often look to Bedford. The chain stores will donate, but they want to know what the local businesses are giving. Bedford often sets the bar—with its own fundraising committee to handle such requests. Other employee groups often participate in events like the Cancer Walk, Relay for Life, and charitable golf tournaments.

Bedford focuses on continued learning. Its training center, which provides a variety of programs and seminars, sees a great deal of use. Classes have included instruction on Bedford's 401(K) plan, various computer programs, estate planning, First

Aid, and how to quit smoking, as well as sales and marketing courses for which participants receive "Bedford University" certificates. A company library put together in recent years holds more than 1,000 books, more than 150 audiotapes, and more than 200 videos. It is probably one of the most complete business libraries in the region.

Most of "what Bedford is" goes on behind the scenes. As in the case of a domestic family, outsiders may see the home or know what kind of work its members do. They might even get a sense of the attitude or tone of the family, but they never really understand or experience that family without being a part of it.

Its unique corporate culture distinguishes Bedford from other companies. General manager Jeff Tschetter dove into the culture in recent years. He feels three factors separate Bedford Industries from other organizations:

First, employees share a sense of ownership in Bedford, and they share the goals of management as well. Their ownership in the success of the company makes them more like partners than employees. They go beyond their job descriptions with a willingness to stay late or come in on weekends when a project demands it. Employees know what they are responsible for, but if something outside their jobs needs doing, they are willing to go ahead and do it anyway. As Ludlow has said, "A structure will find itself." Developing jobs around people is largely unnecessary, as a get-it-done attitude supersedes black-and-white job descriptions. Likewise, awareness of who reports to whom falls into place. Bedford is a natural, flowing company in which direction and supervision self-evolve.

Second, Bedford's management does not provide for individual territory. While the company is organized in terms of function—engineering, production, and accounting, for example—the borders between these functions are gray. Bedford's workers constantly cross-function; for instance, those in production engage with engineering in designing equipment. Bedford has founded, if not institutionalized, its strength on this concept.

Third, the members of an inner group of longtime employees remain connected by a Bedford bond that runs deep. Many of them have weathered three-quarters of the Bedford story. They have carried on traditions, passed on stories, and shared wisdom. They are the core of Bedford's chemistry, and they share the will to keep that culture alive.

I

Evolution

1

Imagine

The city of Worthington rests on the edge of Lake Okabena. This lake gave its name to an apple grafted in a large orchard on its south shore in the early 1900s, and the city named H. J. Ludlow "the giver of the Okabena apple to the world." He was also father to a line of innovators and entrepreneurs.

Bedford Industries is rooted deep in a family history and heritage of entrepreneurship. Robert Ludlow's great-uncle, Dwight, founded the Ludlow Greenhouse, now known as Flower Lane. His father, Bedford Ludlow, contributed to Worthington's designation of "Turkey Capital of the World" as the manager of a large turkey farm and as a founding member of the Worthington Dehydrating Company. On the other side of the family, Robert's great-grandfather, Salathiel Bedford, was one of the founders of the First National Bank of Rushmore (later reorganized as the Rushmore State Bank) and a state senator. These people instilled in Robert Ludlow a natural tendency towards entrepreneurship.

Robert Ludlow was born in Wausau, Wisconsin, in 1929 and spent most of his young life in Worthington. After graduation from high school, he attended the University of Minnesota, in Minneapolis, interrupting his formal education to serve in the U.S. Air Force during the Korean Conflict. After receiving an honorable discharge, he returned to the University of Minnesota and graduated in 1954 with a bachelor's degree in agricultural economics.

Patricia Snyder was born and raised in Elmore, Minnesota. Planning to become a kindergarten teacher, she attended the Miss Woods School for Teachers in Minneapolis. Bob and Patricia met on a double date with their best friends. That evening they realized they had met before, though neither remembered the meeting. Finding they had much in common, they married in 1954 and moved back to Worthington. Patricia began teaching; Bob and his father became partners in a turkey farm.

Bob Ludlow is fond of quoting a Chinese proverb—"I'd rather be lucky than smart." He attributes much of his success to being in the right place at the right time. While to some extent this may be the case, other personal qualities, often reflected in the attitudes of Bedford employees, ensured his success.

First is his insatiable desire to learn. He often asks employees, "What did you learn today?" Learning something new each day is one of the habits he values most. This is evident in his own life as he often reads several books at a time. He challenges his employees not only to learn but also to dream up new ideas and to be persistent with them. As Bob's son Peter Ludlow has written, "He taught me about having at least one new idea every day and how to stay with each new idea, sometimes for years, reworking it until it came to fruition."

Bob Ludlow does not expect success in everything he tries. Many of his ideas, including that of the twist tie, might more easily have failed than not. Peter Ludlow said, "He also taught me that one has to expect a high rate of failure among radical ideas." Potential failure did not stop Bob—sometimes it provided even greater motivation.

In 1957, when Bob Ludlow chose to leave the turkey business, he joined Raven Industries, Inc., out of Sioux Falls. Raven manufactured hot-air balloons and other products in the aerospace industry. Most of its sales and experiments were for government purposes. But Ludlow, as assistant sales manager and marketing analyst, was in charge of sales and product development for the commercial and industrial divisions. His area included products made from plastic film (other than balloons), foam, and fiberglass.

According to Russ Pohl, former senior scientist at Raven and close friend of Bob Ludlow, he and Ludlow were involved in projects that pushed their boundaries and made them think in

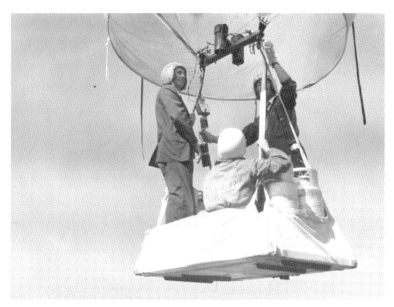

Bob Ludlow stood at the edge of the basket
on a Raven Industries balloon flight.

new ways. In recent years, much attention has been given to the attempts and accomplishments of hot-air-balloon pilots trying to fly around the world. When Pohl and Ludlow were with Raven, the firm did circumnavigate the globe with unmanned super-pressure balloons carrying classified payloads. But the general public knows little of their accomplishment because, until very recently, the project was classified. The firm also flew helium balloons carrying mice to altitudes of 100,000 to 120,000 feet. This project proved humans could survive in space too.

Another project at Raven was the creation of a five-million-candlepower flare for use on balloons. As Pohl has said, "If you set one off over Sioux Falls, you could read a newspaper from anywhere in the city." As to providing balloons for *The Great Race*, Pohl crowed, "We even got into the movies!"

Raven set out to find a way to store natural gas underground. The project site was about 200 feet below the plains of Kansas, where Ludlow helped test the plastic structures under development. He recalled going down into the structure through pipes that were to be sealed and pressurized. It was a tight squeeze. When he entered, a miner from West Virginia told him he must not panic if anything happened. With panic, the body swells, and they would not be able to get him out.

In 1964, Bob Ludlow went to work for the Griffolyn Company, Inc., a firm that reinforced polyethylene film for the sides of trailer homes. During his two years with Griffolyn, sales doubled, but Bob had to travel from home during most of the week. While the Ludlows and their two young children were ready to move to Houston, Bob realized that he wanted to start his own business. He did not want to work for someone else.

The most difficult part of starting his own business was trying to find a market that he could enter with relative ease. "It took two years to find something good," Ludlow recalled, "something I could really do."

During those two years, Bob made some decisions that shaped the beginning of Bedford Industries. The first was the Ludlows' decision to move back to Worthington, where he had lived most of his life. Bob and Patricia began waiting for a house they could afford to become available on Lake Okabena. When one did go up for sale, "We traded another lot we had as a down payment because we couldn't do it any other way."

While Ludlow now lived in Worthington, he continued to travel out of Sioux Falls for Griffolyn. About this time Bob and Pat visited close friends Gordy and Phyl Almberg at a fish house on Lake Okabena. Phyl had brought along a bag of bread for sandwiches—closed with a paper-and-asphalt twist tie. Bob looked at the tie and said, "I can do that, and I can do it better."

The packaging industry was just beginning to put twist ties on plastic bags and garbage bags. At first there were only paper ties, like the ones Ludlow encountered. Plas-Ties Corporation (a division of Royal Industries) and DuPont were the exceptions; they had started to produce a few plastic versions. Ludlow envisioned this as "the ultimate in packaging convenience," but he believed he could improve it. Burford machines, developed to apply twist ties to bread bags in bakeries, often tore the paper ties apart. Another drawback was that most ties had a quarter-inch of wire protruding from the end, due to shrinkage of paper or plastic. Ludlow believed he could correct both problems.

On another front, Bob learned from his cousin, Tom Ludlow, an employee of Bemis Company, Inc., in Minneapolis, that Tom's firm was considering the manufacture of twist tie as well. Bob waited to see what Bemis would do. When he saw his cousin a month or two later, he learned that Bemis had decided not to enter the field. This was the break in the market he had been looking for.

Ludlow knew what he was getting into. He had learned to figure manufacturing costs and selling prices from his work at Raven Industries. "I sat on an airplane and worked out my whole business scenario on a slide rule," he said. The wealth of knowledge built from learning and problem solving at his previous jobs was beginning to pay off.

Soon Bob had learned enough, and the market was opening perfectly for the creation of a new product. The expanding twist-tie market was accompanied by a growing industry of bread and garbage bags. Prices were high because large companies had entered the business and they all had large price margins. DuPont, American Can Company, and Plas-Ties were major producers.

Ludlow described his entry into the business: "You have everything you need—high-priced competitors, poor quality, and expanding markets. You get a chance to get in there, develop your technology, make your mistakes, and learn everything. Nobody pays attention to you because the market is expanding, and they have nice margins all the time." He planned to operate in the shadow of the higher-profile companies—to develop his manufacturing processes and correct his mistakes—then come out as the low-cost supplier. The current market scenario gave him some time, providing a prime opportunity to achieve these goals.

In 1965 the twist-tie industry was relatively small but growing (see "A Twist of Hisotry" in the appendix for more details). The Burford Corporation was the driving force behind the twist tie in the bakery market. The company had an array of four automatic Tyer machines meant for in-line placement at wholesale bread bakeries. Burford Corporation was also the main distribu-

THE MEYER'S SUCCESS STORY

Loving Care
and a
Twist-Tie

Jerry Winer, Mgr., Meyer's Bakery of Hope, Ark.

How do you become Number One in the industry like Meyer's Bakeries in Arkansas? You start with a quality product (and don't spare the loving care). Add a clean, strong package...and a Twist-Tie. President Charles Meyer, Jr. said "Our plants changed to Burford Twist-Tie equipment after using two other closure systems. Twist-Ties are easy to handle. The housewife simply twists to open, twists to close. Her package is reusable and she has a ribbon-premium for many uses around the home."

Burford has a Twist-Tie system for your plant—we'd like to show it to you.

JOIN THE LEADERS! More than 800 production plants from coast to coast rely on fast, dependable Burford Twist-Tie equipment. Mail today for more information.

Name_____
Company_____ Title_____
Address_____
City_____ State_____

BURFORD DISTRIBUTING CORP.
* DISTRIBUTORS OF BURFORD PACKAGING EQUIPMENT
SUITE 900 · EXCHANGE BANK & TRUST BLDG.
EXCHANGE PARK · DALLAS, TEXAS 75235

T. M.   T. M. OF BURFORD CO., INT.

An article in the Burford Corporation's newsletter–
Tie Times–September 1965.

tor of DuPont's Tybex, a plastic "easy-open, easy-close twist-tie ribbon." Package Containers, Inc., of Portland, Oregon, was another major player. It made paper Insta-Tie Ribbon. Both companies had seven available colors, and Package Containers could also produce ties with foil paper, printing, and dating. These original companies pushed the industry, but they left a lot of room for improvement. The ties from both manufacturers came with exposed-wire problems because of the poor adhesion from the wire to the paper or plastic. Ludlow thought that if he could solve this adhesion problem, the bakeries would insist on his product.

In January 1966, Ludlow decided to get into the twist-tie industry. He had accumulated $13,000, mostly through stock options at Raven. He could use that to finance the start of his business. Patricia, previously a kindergarten teacher in Worthington, had two young children at home and did not want to go back to work. Despite the lack of a second-income safety net, the Ludlows decided to try it.

"It takes a special type of wife to withstand the pressures and not let daily fears dominate your life," Bob said. The bank needed a guarantee from the Ludlows before Bedford could borrow any money. Patricia had to cosign all notes. She was signing away her home, its contents, and even the clothes off her back, should the company fail. "It's a pressure that few women with-

This small green garage on the south beltline of Worthington served as the first Bedford Industries factory.

stand because the risks far outweigh the rewards," Bob remarked. But Patricia shared the vision and had faith in what they could achieve.

The first thing the Ludlows did was order stationery for writing inquiry letters. They kept news of the business quiet for a few months, in case it did not work out. They did not tell even Bob's

THERMOPLASTIC EQUIPMENT CORPORATION
DESIGNERS AND BUILDERS OF SPECIALIZED EQUIPMENT FOR THE EXTRUSION INDUSTRY.

VALLEY ROAD • STIRLING, NEW JERSEY 07980 • (201) MITCHELL 3-4600 • (212) CORTLAND 7-6220 • TWX 201-647-4390

January 13, 1966

Mr. Robert Ludlow
P.O. Box 62
Worthington, Minnesota

Dear Mr. Ludlow: Re: TEQ-4697

It was a pleasure meeting you here today, and I would
like to apologize again for the interruptions we had.

Enclosed please find a quotation covering all of the
equipment which we discussed today. As I mentioned to
you, we will set up the complete line in our shop and
give you a demonstration run for your approval.

Should you have any further questions in regard to the
equipment, please don't hesitate to call on me.

                    Very truly yours,

                    THERMOPLASTIC EQUIPMENT CORP.

                    Walter Berlinghof
                    Vice-President

WB/db
Encl: Quotation
cc: J. M. DuPont

*A letter from Walter Berlinghof, vice president of Thermoplastic
Equipment Corporation. Ludlow visited him to look at
and lease Bedford's first extruder.*

own mother. When Patricia went to the bus depot to pick up the stationery, she ran into her mother-in-law and sister-in-law, who were there buying bus tickets. She did not reveal to them the contents of her large box.

Without an operating business, Ludlow was unable to get bank loans. So he traveled to Thermoplastic Equipment Corpo-

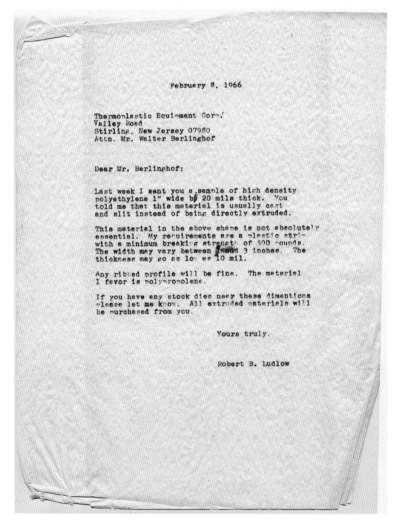

February 8, 1966

Thermoplastic Equipment Corp.
Valley Road
Stirling, New Jersey 07980
Attn. Mr. Walter Berlinghof

Dear Mr. Berlinghof:

Last week I sent you a sample of high density polyethylene 1" wide by 20 mils thick. You told me that this material is usually cast and slit instead of being directly extruded.

This material in the above shape is not absolutely essential. My requirements are a plastic strip with a minimum breaking strength of 500 pounds. The width may vary between 1 and 3 inches. The thickness may go as low as 10 mil.

Any ribbed profile will be fine. The material I favor is polypropolene.

If you have any stock dies near these dimentions please let me know. All extruded materials will be purchased from you.

Yours truly.

Robert B. Ludlow

Ludlow's reply to Walter Berlinghof about testing resin on the Thermoplastic extruder.

ration in New Jersey and leased an extruder—a machine that coats wire with plastic. After leasing the extruder, Bob hired Garold Jenkins as the first employee. Jenkins had been a hired hand on the Ludlow family farm for about 25 years. Ludlow took the extruder, bought some wire from United States Steel Corporation (U.S. Steel), and rented half of a garage on the outskirts of town. Pat set up an office at home to take calls and orders. Then Bedford went to work on the product Ludlow had been dreaming up over the past months—a plastic-coated wire tie, "Tie-Tites."

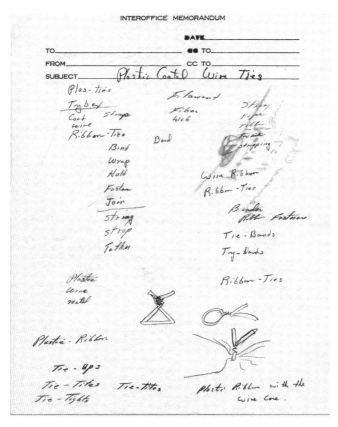

Bob Ludlow made these notes while brainstorming the name Tie-Tites. He dropped the name after a few years because most people called them "twist ties" and because a competitor sold "Tite Ties."

With only $13,000 to play with, Bedford planned to lease or make all its own manufacturing equipment and to set up a national sales-rep system. The company went for 30 days without a sale while learning to make a better twist tie—without spending all of the $13,000. "The necessity of frugality was good beginning training," Ludlow said. "We did not even buy a hammer without thinking about it for a day!"

The shape of the original Bedford logo suggested the company's first product.

Such was the birth of Bedford Industries, though it did not become an official Minnesota corporation until 1967. Ludlow named the company Bedford because it was an old family name, different but easy to remember. Bob saw it as a tribute to his father, Bedford Ludlow.

Bob and Patricia also chose the name partly because they worried that if the company should fail, they would not want the name Ludlow connected with it. They were concerned enough about the risks to tell their children not to talk about what their father did for a living. Patricia recalled that their son, Peter, was asked to share his father's occupation with his fourth-grade class. He told the teacher he was not supposed to talk about it. The teacher asked Bob and Pat Ludlow at a parent-teacher conference whether Bob was in the FBI!

Daughter Sarah (Ludlow) Milbrandt was seven years old when her parents told her they were going to start Bedford. "First thing I remember was Dad saying that he was going to start his own business, I was really excited because I thought he was going to have this great store," she said. "Then they took me out to the little green garage and said he was going to make twist ties. I was disappointed."

Soon after moving into the small garage, Ludlow hired John Taylor. Taylor owned a motor shop in the small town of Org, but his business was not particularly busy. When Ludlow offered him a job, Taylor said to himself, "Boy, this is a good chance to get out of this business." The offer gave him a chance to try something new and to apply what he had learned about motors.

"We had him do everything with small motors," Ludlow said. Taylor's knowledge and resources became a critical asset to the young company. And Taylor brought with him Bedford's first lathe, "the last South Bend Lathe to come out of the factory without being rationed in World War II," passed on to him by his father.

Starting from scratch made for a long learning process before the first twist tie came off the line. Even with Taylor's knowledge of motors, he was puzzled the first time he saw the extruder. He remembered asking, "What kind of a machine is this?"

"It took us 30 days from the time we got the extruder in until we got the first product out," Ludlow explained. Preparing Bedford's first order of 40 spools, the men had to work half the night because of the waste created in the new process. As Ludlow put it, "We made an awful lot of scrap during those first months."

But the orders came in, and the first spools went out—to Pan-O-Gold Baking Company in Pipestone, Minnesota, and Metz Baking Company in Sioux City, Iowa. Bedford's first invoiced sale went to Better Containers Manufacturing Company in Chicago on June 8, 1966. The total bill was $761.30.

"Didn't think you'd ever make twist tie," Jenkins later told Ludlow. At first, he doubted the operation would make it off the ground. The first month saw several failures, especially in operat-

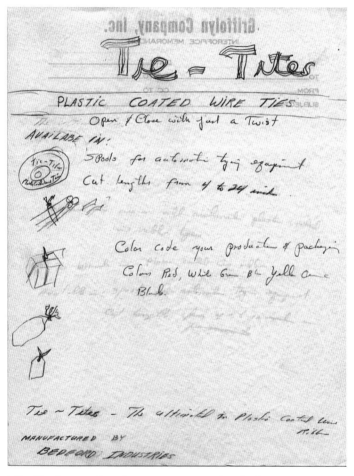

Bob Ludlow's notes from brainstorming Bedford's first brochure, 1966.

ing the new equipment. An extruder melts plastic pellets, called resin, and forms it into a sheet. During the first twist-tie runs the team tried to extrude PVC (polyvinyl chloride) resin. Taylor did not know PVC was unstable at high temperatures, and it caught on fire in the new extruder. To make matters worse, the PVC left hydrochloric acid, so the extruder ended up covered in rust. That put an end to the PVC experiments but did not prevent the team from pressing on.

The first Tie-Tites brochure, February 1967.

Even after the twist-tie product became more consistent, there was much to improve in the process. The quality of wind depended on Garold's skill in winding the tie onto the spool. He used his hands, covered in leather gloves, and an electric drill equipped with an old wooden spool.

"You cut your hands up," Jenkins explained. Leather gloves wore through in two or three hours, so Jenkins eventually replaced the gloves with rags. As employee Doyle Moore described it, "That was a big expense, to buy leather gloves by the boxful." Jenkins remembered that the drills burned out too: "They're not made to run continuously." To remedy this, Taylor found a way to adapt washing machine engines for spooling, which eliminated the need for a drill.

Taylor built most of the Bedford machines out of prepunched iron, much like that in an erector set. This made for easy assembly but often left the equipment unstable—it moved and twisted, compromising the quality of spooling and breaking the wire. But the problems often led to opportunity. The wire breakage created too many short spools. The purchase of a wire chopper allowed Bedford to make cut ties, offering these ties as another product and saving on waste. This left Jenkins with the problem of figuring out how to catch the twist ties emerging from the wire chopper. Painstakingly, he bundled and tied them by hand.

Once the team knew that it could create a strong product, Ludlow set out to form a nationwide distribution network so Bedford could sell in volume. Ludlow's method was fairly easy and, in the long run, successful. Traveling to larger cities, he used the Yellow Pages to find and call wholesale bakeries. He always asked these bakers the location of their headquarters. He went to a city like New York, which had three or four large wholesale bakeries headquartered downtown, then made an appointment with an agent in the purchasing department of each. He took a spool of tie into the purchasing agent and said he was not trying to sell anything. He explained that he had a new product, less expensive than the others on the market, and wanted the names of two or three independent sales representatives from whom the baker purchased supplies. He wanted representatives who could evaluate his product in the bakery lines.

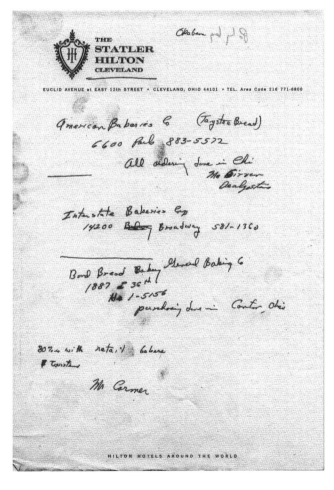

Bob Ludlow's notes from a makeshift hotel-room office in Cleveland.

Often a name came up more than once. Ludlow made the contact, telling the rep that he had been recommended by the bakery he supplied. Ludlow explained that he was trying to sell a product but that he wanted to have it tested—his livelihood and reputation depended on selling a *good* product. He provided the rep with a few spools in return for an evaluation of quality. The rep could easily get the product tested in the bakery—a difficult task for an outsider. When the bakery engineers tested the spools of twist tie, it worked well and was of higher quality than the competition's.

"Half my sales problem was already taken care of before I even tried to make a sale," said Ludlow. When the sales reps came back with positive evaluations, he had a product tested and approved by bakeries, plus connections with purchasing agents who recommended which tie to buy. "I would call the company headquarters and say I had tested my product properly in their bakery and that the purchasing agents and production managers liked it. 'There is no reason now not to have us start supplying some of your baking plants.'" Ludlow could quote a lower price, and almost by default, the bakeries started buying the product from Bedford. The strategy worked well across the country.

One of the representatives recommended to Ludlow was Dick Rohwedder, a packaging salesman. He worked as an engineer for General Bakery but left when the company was sold. Rohwedder was no foreigner to innovation in the bakery industry. On July 7, 1928, his father, Otto Rohwedder, revolutionized the bakery industry with the bread-slicing machine. Dick and Otto traveled to Chillicothe, Missouri, where Frank Bench, a baker on the verge of bankruptcy, was willing to take a chance on the invention. "When no one else in the world would give my father's machine a try, Frank Bench did. Other bakers scoffed at

28

the idea," Dick said. "Frank Bench's bakery increased bread sales by 2,000 percent in two weeks." Sliced bread was an instant success.

Almost 15 years later for Rohwedder, Bedford's twist tie was "the best thing since sliced bread." He picked up the twist tie along with other packaging products he was representing. He saw potential for the twist tie and began committing a majority of his time to Bedford, later becoming a full-time employee. Working in the bakery industry on the East Coast, he was an asset in that location and in teaching Bedford how to sell to that industry.

Bedford's new production center, earlier a hatchery.

In 1968, Bedford Industries expanded from the original garage to an old hatchery building about a block down the street. It had seven employees, and it kept the garage as a machine shop. The office was in the basement of the Ludlows' home, and Patricia was the secretary. In this home office, she answered the phone and handled the billing and payroll. Bedford soon grew out of that office, hiring Karla May as secretary when it moved into its new building. This freed Patricia to leave the house occasionally, but she still did most of the bookwork and payroll. Just about this time, Bedford reached its first month of sales over $25,000. Bob told Patricia she could buy two new dresses to celebrate the achievement.

On May 27, 1968, Bedford hired Doyle Moore to spool the twist tie. Moore was hoping for a job where he could go home after a traditional 9-to-5 workday. "When I went to work for Bedford," Moore said, "I told my wife I was going to work at a job where it was 40 hours a week and you could go home." Years later Moore was still putting in well-over-40-hour weeks. In the year before his retirement, Moore recalled just two weeks in which he worked just 40 hours.

Later in 1968, Bedford searched for a polychemist to employ as a plastics engineer. Several large manufacturing companies were experiencing layoffs, so Ludlow called USI Company to see whether it had any engineers who specialized in plastics. Ludlow met Tom Haddock at O'Hare Airport in Chicago. They talked about the problems Bedford faced with the twist tie and how they could be corrected. Ludlow brought John Taylor's notes from previous experiments and asked Haddock to look them over. The suggestions that Ludlow brought back from Chicago created a plastic blend that Bedford then used for years.

Haddock started work at Bedford the Monday before Thanksgiving 1968. "That afternoon Ludlow handed him a plane ticket and told him to go home," Doyle Moore remembered. Haddock thought his job was short-lived, but Ludlow told him that he needed to be with his family for Thanksgiving. "Yeah, worked one whole day before he was told to go home," Moore said. "I think Barb [Haddock] thought you went to work for a nut!"

Haddock recalled going to Ludlow's office one day to say he thought that Doyle Moore was a talent not being used for what he had to offer. A week later, Moore was reporting directly to Tom. This was the beginning of one of Bedford's more colorful and successful teams. Haddock described his and Moore's relationship as simpatico—he could be thinking that he needed a screwdriver, and Doyle would hand one to him.

"We made our equipment out of whatever we could find," Moore said. They had no other choice because Bedford was running on a shoestring budget. The engineers often found themselves at the junkyard right across the street. They adopted most of their technology from the farming industry—from feed mixers to level winders to brake drums. Even if Bedford had the money, it was useless for the company to order equipment. "You could buy cams, you could order them, but it took six months to get them," Moore said. "By that time, the way we made stuff and the way we changed it, it would have changed long before you got them."

"I used to put machines together with vise grips," explained Moore. Ludlow often told the engineers that Bedford was more sophisticated than Raven because Raven built machines with C-clamps. "If we put it together with vise grips and got it working, that's the way it worked," Moore said. At one time Moore had 70-some pairs of vise grips and 36 C-clamps. Ludlow showed the mindset of Bedford engineers in a conversation with Tom and Doyle: "Just keep in mind: this is a prototype machine. The junkyard is across the highway, and Doyle, you can always buy more vise grips at Coast-to-Coast."

Many of the machines built in the late 1960s have been overhauled and are still in use at Bedford today. "They used to give me a bad time about building stuff too heavy, but it's still there," Moore said. In general, industrial machines are engineered to run only eight hours a day. Bedford, however, was running the machines 24 hours a day, six (and occasionally seven) days a week. As Moore put it, preventive maintenance meant building equipment that was strong and solid.

"One weakness we had was that there were no machine shops in the area doing what we needed," Ludlow explained. Bedford had no source other than itself for most of its equipment and parts. The tie industry was so new that production machinery was nonexistent. Except for the extruder and chopper, Bedford built all its own equipment. The Bedford team turned this disadvantage into one of its greatest advantages. The engineers built their own machine shop, which allowed them to continually create and improve equipment. This let's-do-it-ourselves philosophy allowed the company to respond to customers in ways other firms could not.

Building its own machines and developing processes from scratch pushed Bedford ahead and allowed it to learn. Tom and Doyle bought books when they did not know something—but rarely finished reading them. They read as much as they needed to figure out what to do, put the book away, and went on to something new.

"There wasn't too much we couldn't figure out how to do one way or another," Moore said. What they accomplished with limited tools and technology was astounding. The secret, according to John Taylor, was that "we used our imagination."

2

Try anything

One Saturday morning Moore was cleaning up the hatchery building. As he was throwing oil cans into a box, it suddenly went up in flames! He quickly started the forklift and drove the box outside. "Tom [Haddock] and I were cleaning up, just hauling out junk," Moore remembered. "Everything from the hatchery was still in the building, and there was junk all over the place." Moore had not noticed what Haddock had put in the box earlier—a can filled with potassium permanganate, a substance used in chicken feed. "You've got that and oil—and instant fire!" Moore exclaimed. "Before then I had fed it to chickens but never mixed it with oil. Anything for excitement!"

Excitement was the theme for the next few years, resulting in some of Bedford's most memorable stories of success and failure. The key to success was the good chemistry blossoming among employees joining the company.

Employees new and old fostered a philosophy of dedication. Late nights and long weekends were often required because of the speed with which the youthful twist-tie industry was moving.

"I would go home and say I'd be back in four hours," Moore remembered. "I went home, took a shower, slept for three hours, went back to work, and my wife never knew I was there. She was so used to my coming and going that it did not wake her up. If something had to be done, we worked."

Haddock and Moore worked to perfect a spooler that tapered the flanges of a plastic spool. They were close, but as Haddock said, "Success always seemed just one vise grip away." One Friday afternoon, Ludlow told Moore, "I'm going to Metz Baking on Monday, and I need five spools for trial—even one spool would do. But don't work all weekend." Ludlow was ambitious when it came to finishing projects. He was known to say, "There are 24 hours in a day; whichever 24 you want to work is up to you."

Haddock, Moore, and other members of the Bedford team spent many late nights in the Gateway Café, next door to Bedford. Here, drinking coffee and drawing on napkins, they solved problems and dreamed about new ideas. They became so comfortable there that one day the bill was twice as much as normal. Tom asked the owner, "Did you raise your prices?" He replied, "No, you forgot to pay yesterday."

One late-night dilemma involved the consistency of plastic. The buckets for mixing plastic were creating irregularities in the mix. Haddock took a napkin and drew up what he needed to mix the plastic properly. Moore looked at it and said, "All that is, is a feed mixer." They left the Gateway Café for a tour of farm feed mixers at two o'clock in the morning. Using their flashlights to see the equipment, they searched every farming implement store in Worthington. As they crawled back over a fence at the John Deere implement, a light shined back on them. It was Jake Van Hall, a local police officer who went by the nickname Sarge. He said, "Haddock and Moore checking out old equipment. I've never met two guys like you." They all went back to the Gateway Café for coffee.

Although they worked long hours, Haddock and Moore knew when it was time to go home. Once, about 1:00 A.M., Moore was welding a piece of equipment. After finishing, he and Haddock went next door to the Gateway Café. Moore said, "Sure would be a joke if I'd welded that thing at the wrong end." Looking at it more closely, they realized that Moore indeed had welded it incorrectly. They went back to the shop and got the torch to cut it off. Moore cleaned it off, lined it up, and welded it back together—on the same wrong end "That's when we decided to go home," Moore said.

Doyle Moore's children thought he was crazy when he showed them his first paycheck years later, for $1.45 an hour! "I

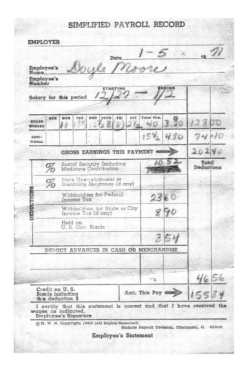

Doyle Moore's early paycheck was enough for a family of eight.

know at one time I had more raises than anybody in the place," he said. "Everybody got a raise every year—a nickel or a dime." One week Ludlow gave him a raise for all the hours he worked. In another week, he got a raise once again. One week later, the yearly raise was given to everybody. Moore received three raises in two weeks—worth 20 cents. As he reflected later, "We raised a family on less money than you pay now for taxes."

Building new machines and looking for ideas at farm implement dealers could not solve all of the problems Bedford Industries faced. In one incident, an old extruder with a water-cooled variable-speed transmission kept shutting off irregularly. If the machine lost water pressure, it stopped running. For a few months, the machine ran fine but shut down sporadically. It might run for few hours or a couple of weeks with no apparent pattern. About 2:00 one morning, Moore was working and went to the rest room. When he flushed the toilet, he heard somebody in the rest room right behind him flush the toilet too. "Right then I knew what it was. If too many people went to the rest room right in a row, it dropped the water pressure and shut the extruder off. We had the most remotely controlled extruder in the industry!"

The Bedford team always looked for new products and ideas. Some ideas had nothing to do with the twist tie. In 1969, Bedford considered manufacturing plastic horseshoes, drinking and stirring straws, and hard plastic tubes used for jump ropes. It even bought a plastic tube-drawing unit to make spray tubes for aerosol cans. None of these ideas made it to Bedford's product line, but the company kept looking for the one that would.

Bedford began to take pride in its ability to create new products and meet the demands of customers. A company from Canada, for instance, was having problems with its packaging and needed specially designed twist tie. Within five hours the

Bedford team made die modifications, ran the tie material, and was on a plane for Canada to hand-deliver and install the twist tie. This type of service, combined with technical knowledge, enabled Bedford to grow in the competitive packaging field. Bedford was developing a reputation for its new products and quick reaction time to customers.

"We built it on service," Moore said. "Didn't matter what it was—somebody had trouble, somebody went to take care of it." At one point, a truck strike prevented Bedford from shipping orders. "Every bus that came through town, we shipped something," Moore recalled. He loaded his old green Dodge van and went to the depot. "I think the bus drivers hated to see us coming. Every bus that came to town, didn't matter what direction it went, we had a customer someplace who needed spools, so we put it on the bus." Because of Bedford's defining class of service, some clients who once received spools by bus are still its loyal customers.

Karla May was the first secretary for Bedford after Patricia Ludlow. She used Bob Ludlow's Underwood typewriter from college until the company finally sprang for an IBM. The man

*"Miss Twistee" appeared on Bedford envelopes
and in a few advertisements.*

who came to service the IBMs ran speed-typing contests and guaranteed that no one could jam one. But Karla May typed so fast she not only jammed it but also made the type ball fly out. She seldom made a typo and never comprehended what she typed until she proofread it. Haddock and Moore once filled out a purchase order with the words "One basket of money" in the middle. "You could hear her scream across the plant," Haddock said.

Norma Jacobs (later Norma Cook) came to Bedford in May 1969. She was looking for a secretarial job, and one of her high-school teachers lined up an interview for her at Bedford. She wondered, "What is Bedford? Where is it?" After her interview with Bob Ludlow, he asked whether she could begin the next day. She started the day before high-school graduation. She had never held a job off her family's farm, so the first day was intimidating. Answering her first phone call—from Dick Rohwedder—threw her off because she did not know what to do or how to spell his name.

John Van Ede worked as a truck driver for Cashway Lumber. Previously employed by a manufacturing company in Mankato, he had vowed never to work in manufacturing again. But when he dropped off a load of lumber in Worthington for Ron White, a Bedford employee, White told him about Bedford Industries and how it manufactured twist ties. Intrigued with the business, Van Ede decided to stop by Bedford on his way out of town. He walked in and asked for a supervisor. Bob Ludlow offered to show him around, but Van Ede was unaware he was the owner. A few weeks later, Ludlow asked Van Ede to come and work for Bedford. Van Ede was impressed enough to break his vow.

Karla May and Norma did all of Bedford's communication by hand, with the typewriter and carbon copies. John Van Ede wrote each production run by hand, and Norma typed the orders. Despite all the typing, Karla and Norma brought books to read because they occasionally ran out of paperwork. But over all, Bedford was busy. In 1971 the company reached monthly sales of $100,000. The employees held a party with cake and ice cream to celebrate this monumental achievement.

Three years after Bedford hit $100,000 in sales, the Worthington Daily Globe ran this photo with the following caption: "Bedford Industries, Inc., Worthington, Minnesota, is an extruder of plastic products. Distributed nationally, the plastic-coated wire ties are manufactured for use in consumer convenience packaging. Robert B. Ludlow (left), President, Bedford Industries, shows a proprietary line of plastic tie ribbon to Harry N. Dirks (right), President, First National Bank of Worthington."

About 12 twist-tie manufacturers existed in the nation and Bedford was among the three smallest. The company had only about 20 employees, a few single-wire lines, and a couple of spoolers. Bedford had a lot of work to do if it wanted to catch up with the industry leader—Plas-Ties.

In 1971, Lloyd Tinklenberg came to Worthington. Lloyd was searching for a job because his wife, Connie, had been hired by the local school system. He asked around town about Bedford Industries, but no one seemed to know much, so he decided to stop by. "I walked in, and I'm standing at the counter talking to Karla May, explaining to her I have an engineering degree, and I'm kind of looking around for something. I'm curious about what you do."

He was soon shown into Ludlow's office, then sent on a tour of the plant with Tom Haddock. "Next thing I know there's this short guy with a crew cut showing me around." Lloyd was confused by the machines and spools. After Tom explained that they made twist ties, Lloyd thought, "Oh great, something that nobody thinks about." He went home that night and told Connie, "I found something that seems to be in my field, and I think it has possibilities."

Upon hearing that Bedford made twist ties, she said, "You better keep looking—nobody's going to make a living selling twist ties." Three days later Lloyd received a phone call: Would he start the following Monday? He went to work running night shifts and eventually became a driving force for new products—he built Bedford's first in-line printer, used for years to print dates on twist ties.

Soon after Lloyd joined the team, Bedford perfected the paper/plastic tie—"one of the major products that put Bedford on the map." As the engineers were laminating paper, they devel-

*Four faces on the early Bedford team (clockwise from top):
John Van Ede, Lloyd Tinklenberg, Tom Haddock, and Doyle Moore.*

oped the paper/plastic tie combination. Bakeries liked plastic
ties for durability but needed paper ties for printing. A tie with
paper on one side and plastic on the other was perfect.

The product was ready for sale just 18 months after Tom
Haddock's first mock-up. The manufacturing process was slow,
running a mere 15 feet of tie per minute. "We'd stand there, a
whole shift waiting for a 6,000-foot run," Lloyd remembered.
But once on the market, the paper/plastic ties took the bakery
industry by storm. Phil Merlin, president of Alcar Industries,
later told Ludlow that he thought Alcar was going to fail in the
baking industry until it created its own paper/plastic ties.

Bedford's twist-tie market was becoming too large for Dick
Rohwedder to handle alone, so Bob needed another salesperson.

Ted Ludlow, Bob's younger brother, was in a management position at a company in Grand Rapids that recently had been sold and might leave Ted looking for a new opportunity. The sales position was a good fit for Ted, and it was a good time for him to join Bedford.

Ted believes teamwork was and is the key to Bedford's success. "We went through all the learning curves. But there was an incredible sense of teamwork: in production, sales, engineering, and by the guys in the shop who were making parts for us. We were getting this stuff turned around in hours and days—it didn't stretch into weeks and months. I think people were working really hard and having a whale of a lot of fun. I can remember my favorite day of the week was Monday—because I had five days of work ahead of me."

In 1971 Bedford marked its entrance into the garbage-bag market with the gang tie—a perforated sheet of ties. The gang tie, with the paper/plastic combination, was a product that trash-bag and food-packaging producers were searching for. Consumers no longer had to rummage through a box of trash bags to find twist ties—they could simply pull one off the gang-tie sheet. The tie was rust resistant, allowing food packagers to enjoy the advantages of the twist tie. Bedford acquired two dozen substantial clients and major accounts, including Union Carbide Corporation and Mobil Chemical Company. Mobil Chemical sales alone comprised 20 percent of Bedford's business.

Though it was no easy task to manage 50 wires and a hot glue pot, John Van Ede mastered operation of the gang-tie machine, an extruder combined with a multiwire laminator—which was a step forward for Bedford. Due to its complexity, the gang-tie machine was one of the few that Bedford did not build itself. But it served as a model for Bedford's engineers to duplicate.

42

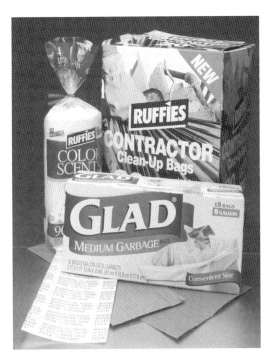

*Bedford gang-tie products had many practical applications.
Both GLAD® and Ruffies jumped on the possibilities.*

Union Carbide, one of Bedford's largest accounts, wanted
Bedford to consider some special applications. The client envisioned a consumer purchasing a turkey in a grocery store, taking
it home, and putting it in the oven without removing the turkey
from the bag. Union Carbide wanted an "ovenable" twist tie. To
find an adhesive that could withstand oven temperatures, Tom
Haddock focused on the problem two days. He came up with an
answer—liquid glass, which is also used to glue foil to cigarette
packages.

There was one problem—the adhesive required a five-foot-
long dryer in the middle of the brand new tie line. The new tie
line had spent a year in the making, and Bedford had only recently begun profiting from it. Much to Ludlow and Van Ede's

dismay, Moore and Haddock were ready to cut the machine in half. The operation worked, and Bedford was able to accommodate Union Carbide's request. A couple of days later, Haddock was in a coffee shop downtown. The patrons asked why Bob Ludlow had seemed disturbed when he came in two days earlier. Haddock knew it was because he had cut the new tie line in half.

Bedford set its sights on another breakthrough—the all-plastic, wireless twist tie. "It's hilarious really, looking back," Haddock reflected years later. The idea started when Lloyd Tinklenberg had an idea for dog-food bags—a tie strung with fishing line. When the consumer pulled on the fishing line, the tie both shut the bag and sealed it. Pulling in the opposite direction reopened the bag. It was a reclosure solution for dog-food companies that inspected bags with a metal detector, which meant they could not use metal twist ties. The Bedford team decided that a better solution was a twist tie made only of plastic.

Fishing line from a local hardware store powered the first attempt to replace the steel wire. But the line was too short and too weak. Ludlow decided to purchase heavy-duty fishing line direct from the manufacturer—Berkeley in Spirit Lake, Iowa. Bedford bought 50 thousand-foot spools of fishing line. The engineers ran the heavy fishing line, making a gang of five ties, and spooled it. The blue tie looked beautiful on the eight-inch plastic spool. Finishing on a Friday afternoon, Haddock placed three spools on his desk and left for the weekend.

When he returned on Monday, the spools of wireless tie had been sabotaged. There was tie and broken spool all over his office. "I went looking for someone to kill," Haddock said. After walking around the building to find the culprit, Haddock got Moore to join him for a closer look. Both men agreed that the broken spools looked as if they had been crushed. After more

44

consideration, they came to a different conclusion—the fishing line had shrunk so much that it destroyed the spool!

The team tried anything that offered the slightest possibility, including rolls of polypropylene fiber and plain string. As much as Bedford wanted to invent the wireless twist tie, it could not find the magic ingredients. Due to limited funds and time, the project had to become a dream for the future. "I admire Bob for how patient he was with everything that happened," John Van Ede said. "He was never upset when things failed. His only response: 'Well, what did you learn?'"

3

Innovate

B edford's corporate image became the definition of speed, service, and quality. By 1971 the company was a strong force in the twist-tie market—no longer insignificant in the industry, it was maturing. With an impressive factory and a rapidly growing customer list, Bedford Industries could be described as successful after being in business only five years. Ludlow described its success as "a little luck, a great deal of vision, and a lot of hard work." These characteristics steered the company through change, propelling Bedford into the future.

The 14,000-square-foot hatchery building could no longer contain Bedford's growth. In 1971, Bedford employees began designing a new state-of-the-art headquarters and manufacturing facility to fulfill their future goals. Ludlow said, it was "designed by our own people and best fit the processes of our operation." They incorporated the latest in labor- and energy-saving devices, including a unique heat-utilization system. The system recaptured the heat from the extruding process, using it to heat the entire production floor through the cold Minnesota winters.

The frame of the new Rowe Avenue facility began to take shape, 1973.

Bedford worked with the City of Worthington throughout 1972 to secure industrial-revenue bonds to aid in the construction of the new factory. A location was chosen, and construction began on the north side of Worthington in early 1973. The new facility provided 30,000 square feet of manufacturing space, 1,000 square feet for offices, 1,000 square feet for a laboratory, and 1,000 square feet for engineering.

In April 1973, Ludlow was in the Minneapolis area looking for an accountant. Connecting through an employment agency, Bob Ludlow and Bob Boushek found a chemistry that was right for Bedford. "I used to work for Sheldahl [Inc.] in Northfield, which was also in the balloon business. It was dear to Bob's [Ludlow's] heart because he had been at Raven," Boushek said. Raven and Sheldahl were basically competitors. "I met with Bob and began talking about all the similarities we had. I was out looking because I was dead-ended at Sheldahl. So we kind of clicked. I started working for Bedford in April of '73, which at that time had fewer than 40 employees."

Several technological leaps gave Bedford a competitive advantage. One was the development of the double-wire twist tie, as Bedford's competition extruded only a single-wire twist tie. Haddock and Moore designed the equipment to accomplish the process. They built the press quickly–in only 30 days–and that equipment was still in use some 30 years later.

Keebler wanted to use the double-wire tie for packaging and pushed Bedford to accomplish the project. "That was a real big plus because that got us into the cracker market and into the cookie-bag market," Ludlow said. "It's difficult, and few competitors attempted it." Keebler especially liked Bedford's paper/ plastic combination on the double-wire tie. Glue could be applied to the paper side to adhere to the bag.

Although the double-wire twist tie was a success, adding more wires did not make a better product. An eight-wire twist tie was a possible solution for the dog-food bag. Haddock and Moore found a way to make it, but the product never gained popularity.

Bedford employees and members of the Worthington City Council dedicated the new factory in October 1973.

The new facility on Rowe Avenue was completed by October 1973. "I don't believe we should have built such a large building—we will never fill it," Bob Ludlow said to Tom Haddock and Doyle Moore as the men gazed across the new production floor. The 33,000-square-foot building more than doubled the size of the previous factory. It appeared to be more than Bedford could ever need.

The Worthington Daily Globe ran the photo above with this caption: "Two new local industries to hold open house: City and state officials were on hand in Worthington's North Industrial Park this morning for the formal dedication of two new industries. Gunter Fuhrmannek (left) is holding golf clubs produced by American Precision Golf Co. Robert Ludlow (right), president of Bedford Industries, Inc., displays spools of the plastic ties produced here for industrial and commercial use. Both industries are 'homegrown,' and both now ship products to a worldwide market." (Jim Brandenburg photo)

Bedford was not the only young company in town with an exciting product. Gunter Fuhrmannek, a tool-and-die machinist who previously worked for Ping, came to Worthington to start American Precision Golf Company. The *Worthington Daily Globe* featured Bedford and American Precision Golf, both of which held open houses to show their new facilities to the community.

A feature section on the two companies ran in the *Globe* on May 23, 1974. It celebrated the achievements of Bedford Industries and the grand opening of its new factory. It also commented on Bedford's innovation and people. In part:

> Innovation and diversification are the watchwords of Bedford, a comparatively infant firm with only six years of production history. "We have to constantly improve over present products, and we have to look for international markets," says Ludlow. "This is the nature and demand of our market."
>
> Watchwords have proven true: Bedford Industries produces a tie closure that is unlike any in the industry. Its methods, its locally produced machinery, are trade secrets. The employees, who are developers of the plant's expanding product, jealously guard the exclusive designs they utilize in their manufacturing that has made them "one of the largest in the industry."
>
> At times Ludlow says he comes across his ties on unexpected packages. "We're diversified across so many different markets that I often have no idea what a customer wants to use the ties for," he says. "Each market has a different sales technique, and that's constant change, constant innovation."
>
> The success of Bedford Industries is more than a tribute to its president, Bob Ludlow. It is an example of employee loyalty and the optimistic backing of the community. The present plant was financed through community-backed industrial revenue bonds. "Without Worthington's support it wouldn't have been possible," says Ludlow, who quickly adds that the community's signature on the bank note is virtually liability-free.

But the single most important ingredient is people: Dedicated people. Bedford has captured a small, select hunk of the rapidly expanding packaging industry. Their formula for success has been innovation, the kind of innovation possible when people—employees—seek to improve their product. "We'll last as long as we can maintain constant innovation," Ludlow observes. "When we lag in technology we die."

About the time the new plant opened, the bakery industry had accumulated a surplus of empty plastic spools and had few ways to get rid of them. The spools mounted in the bakeries, resulting in wasted space and added expense. Bedford sought to eliminate this problem through a campaign prompting bakeries to "Turn a Profit! With your empty Bedford tie-ribbon plastic spools":

Bakeries have been converting their empty Bedford Tie Ribbon plastic spools into profit by converting them to "trim" or "exercising" wheels and selling them in their bread surplus outlets. One Midwestern bakery sold 500 such converted spools in a period of three months through one outlet.

It took only minutes for one of their maintenance personnel to nail in six painted sticks and put a dowel in the center hole. The picture shows a string attached to the wheel; this is for the purpose of hanging the wheels on display. The salesgirls in the store are enthusiastic about these slenderizing wheels and do a good job of "talking it up" to the customers.

"Exercising-wheels" or "trim-wheels" are being advertised in the major stores at $5.95. The bakery outlet sold them at $1 and the demand exceeds supply. These wheels build traffic!

In case you haven't noticed the advertisements, the wheel is placed on the floor in front of you with one hand on each side of the handle. The advertisements claim that pushing forward and back a dozen times per day will trim the waistline. The housewife buys this.

Another way to take a throwaway item in your plant and turn it into a profitable traffic-builder. Have you maintenance department make up a few wheels today!

The campaign did not last long because Bedford soon conceived a product eliminating plastic spools. A national oil shortage was causing long lines at gas stations and, because plastic is derived from oil, skyrocketing plastic prices. Spool manufacturers could not get the plastic they needed, so Bedford had to find another way.

Salesman Dick Rohwedder saw a roll of "spoolless tie" on the loading dock of a large bakery. The twist tie was not on a plastic spool—it was wound in a way that held its own circular shape. Alcar Industries created the new method, and Bedford believed spoolless tie could be the future.

The Bedford team went to work and emerged with a process using textile-winding techniques. Bedford's "precision-wound tie" eliminated the plastic spool, holding a round shape on a paper core with fewer breaks and snags. It required the development of a special adapter because application machinery in the bakeries was built for plastic spools.

The entire project took a few months and a lot of learning. Doyle Moore had to learn trigonometry, for example. Nobody had taught him trig before, so Tom Haddock worked with him and, in a few days, he designed the spool adapter. He developed many designs before Bedford decided which one to patent.

Bedford needed to know its market for the spoolless tie. Ludlow called the Burford Corporation and asked how many twist-tie machines existed in bakeries. "They told me 500," Ludlow said. "I figured that was good market research." Moore said it was the worst prediction Ludlow ever made—Bedford ended up producing thousands of spool adapters.

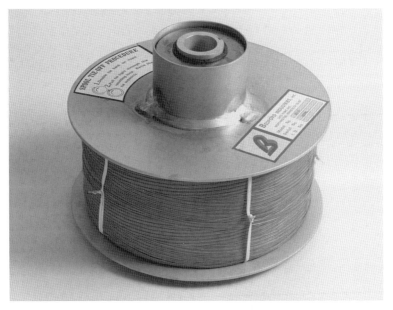

A roll of Bedford's precision-wound tie, installed on a spool adapter.

The precision-wound tie and spool adapter, tested in a few bakeries, received outstanding reviews. The technology was superior to anything the bakeries had used earlier because the precision wind eliminated the tangling of the old plastic spools. The spoolless tie was even more cost-effective—the paper core was cheaper than the plastic spool. The bakery engineers always asked Lloyd, "Why do you charge less?" The industry demanded Bedford's product, and it met with little competition.

Baking Industry magazine ran an editorial about the Bedford precision-wound technology and spoolless adapter, bringing Bedford numerous sales leads. It said, in part, that the product:

- Increases production efficiency while holding costs in line.
- Precision wound tie ribbon system, which includes a spool adapter, uses spoolless tie ribbon, cuts downtime and lowers cripple rate.
- Taking only 2 minutes to install, spool adapter is fastened to spool shaft or tyer and becomes part of the tyer's braking system.
- Adapter prevents spool slippage, makes tie lengths more uniform, stops ties from slipping down the side of spool and eliminates tie tangles.
- Made by lamination process using plastic adhesive instead of glue, tie ribbon is available in standard widths in all paper, plastic, and plastic-paper ties. Ribbon can be baked, boiled or frozen without altering any of its qualities.

Bedford's spoolless tie and adapter had the competition in an uproar. A few years later, Phil Merlin, president of Alcar Industries, told Bob Ludlow that Alcar had tried the spoolless tie, which Rohwedder saw on the loading dock. Merlin was shocked to hear Bedford was marketing the same product. Bob Whiting, president of Plas-Ties, sent out a concerned sales bulletin to his employees on May 29, 1975:

> Bedford is now promoting a spool without the flange for automatic twist-tie machines and offering a $0.40 discount. Please be sure to keep in touch with your customers to find out if this is a threat to our business and if this "gimmick" appears to be worth $0.40.
>
> Our initial reaction from discussions among ourselves and with customers is negative. First of all, handling of a partially used spool puts a great deal of burden on the operating

people. With a little abuse you could have a handful of "spaghetti" rather than a usable spool of material. Secondly, the twist-tie machine must have a spool adapter supplied by Bedford at a cost of $45.00.

However, Bedford is a respected competitor. This item may be better than we think, so we are testing various winding techniques to be ready for the market if forced upon us. In the meantime, you could help us with any specific product information such as samples or photos of the spool to determine the wind and photos of the spool adapter. Any news would be greatly appreciated.

Don't let Bedford scoop us, so dig in and keep us posted!

"The spoolless tie was what crushed us," Bob Whiting said 30 years later. "The biggest problem for the twist tie in the bakery industry was the wind. We saw Bedford's spoolless tie and said we're not going to spend the money to do the me-too." Bedford realized this product's potential, and it revolutionized the bakery industry. The momentum gained in introducing the new product led to the use in the baking industry of more than 3,000 spoolless adapters by the year 2004.

Combining the spoolless adapter with Bedford's plastic/paper tie sent the company's sales soaring. An article in *Baking Industry* explained the advantages of Bedford's product:

> [Better Krust Bakeries] began using the paper/plastic ties last year when it developed a new line of Country Hearth variety bread to be packaged in 2 mil bags. The company management felt its present tie did not allow for reuse of the bag. The tie also did not provide a tight enough package, as Sunbeam had switched to a heavier bag with the new line of bread.
>
> "We felt we could get a better tie and one which would hold better than the straight paper or plastic one," said James La Flame, plant manager. "And we do get more reuse of the paper/plastic tie than with the previous one. We're able to open and close it better. With the paper/plastic tie the package is really closed; it gives a tight package."

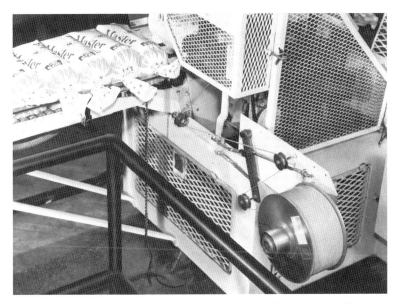

Bakeries nationwide converted Burford machines to handle Bedford plastic/paper tie with spoolless adapters.

"Before we introduced our new line of bread we tested the product with consumers. A by-product of our testing was consumer comments concerning the ties," La Flame said. Reactions were favorable, he said.

Economics was also a factor in changing ties. The spoolless paper/plastic ties cost almost 11 percent less than the all-plastic ones previously used.

La Flame also noted that there has been less maintenance and less downtime on the plant's tying machines since the changeover. "Our operators also prefer to work with the new ties," added La Flame. "The ties make it much easier to thread the machines."

The pace set by Bedford provided it with the upper hand in the industry. "Speed in accomplishing things was our most important asset," Bob Ludlow said. Ted Ludlow was a proficient pilot, so Bedford leased a twin-engine airplane to fly from place to place and convert customers. "I could call on three to four times

Salesman Ted Ludlow flew Bedford's twin-engine Cessna.

as many people," Ted said. In two to three months, Bedford had all its customers—and some of the competition's—converted to the spoolless-tie system. The president of Plas-Ties told Bob and Ted that his company could not keep up with Bedford. Plas-Ties heard about the spoolless system in one state and the next day heard about it in two others.

"Pretty soon we had a solid marketplace, and the rest of them were stuck," Ted said. Plas-Ties and other competitors followed with their own spoolless ties, but it was a scramble. "We always came up with something faster and newer. In the marketplace, speed is the determining factor as to whether you are successful," Ted explained.

Bedford's speed, quality, and customer care, along with concern for each employee, provided its successful corporate philosophy. "Our growth philosophy—of providing the best quality of tie ribbon at a competitive price and servicing each account promptly—has enabled us to become one of the top twist-tie manufacturers in the world," Bob Ludlow said.

II

Revolution

4

Adapt

By 1975, Bedford was producing almost 400,000 miles of twist tie annually, enough to encircle the earth 15 times. Growth was leveling off, and the Bedford team had not had a breakthrough since the spoolless tie. The dreamers wanted new ideas and new markets that would allow Bedford new growth based on the technology it had already invested in.

One asset placing Bedford above other manufacturers was the rapid extrusion process it had perfected. The production of a twist tie involves one continuous plastic extrusion, but Bob Ludlow and Tom Haddock wanted to adapt the process to cut specialty figures. "We start with an idea and a process you can make something with," Ludlow said. "Then we ask, 'What else can we make with this process?'"

One possibility was to confront the downside of injection-molding equipment in the container industry. Injection molding is the process of forcing soft plastic into a mold. Cycle times were slow and the walls of containers were thick—creating an inefficient and expensive product. If Bedford could press plastic with a patterned roller during the extrusion process, it could form the containers efficiently and continuously. The method was similar to that of shaping candy and cookies. It had the potential to be faster, more efficient, and cheaper than injection molding. In 1975, the company started to research thermoforming technology as one approach to the project. Conducting a market research program the following year, the Bedford team looked into the possibilities for thermoforming polyethylene containers, including souffle cups, Cool Whip containers, and margarine tubs.

Bedford's first thermoforming machine for lid forming, 1977.

In 1977, Bedford purchased a Thermoline® thermoforming machine from American Western Company in Phoenix. Thus Bedford produced one of the first thermoformed lines in the country manufactured with a completely integrated extrusion process. Bedford felt that using extrusion technology and its large knowledge base was a step in the right direction. It was entering a market with great, but unknown, growth potential.

The Bedford team had to learn a new technology—that of impression dies. The company worked hard to develop skills, despite production obstacles including design of a thermoformed, nonleaking lid for containers and engineering dies. Bedford had a lot of failures, Ludlow said, but that's what it took to develop a great product. Once the team overcame the "humps of development," Bedford began manufacturing styrene and K-resin lids for paper and plastic cups. It sold the lids through a distribution system to fast-food restaurants and the hospital industry. Bedford could fill short-run orders economically that higher-volume manufacturers could not. This ability attracted some major food-container companies, including Lilly-Tulip of Ohio.

A brand new market brought forth an opportunity. Rigid plastic tubs that housed margarine were thick and expensive. Injection molders had not found a way to make thin-wall products (reducing the amount of plastic). So Bedford would have a clear advantage if it introduced a lightweight, user-friendly product. Bedford considered polypropylene plastic because it was not widely used in the plastics industry and thus was less expensive than other plastics. By thin-walling the container, Bedford could reduce the amount of plastic by almost 50 percent. In applying its thin-wall capabilities to polypropylene resin, Bedford attempted to design an inexpensive, competitive product.

Polypropylene had several benefits over styrene, unrelated to price. Both plastics were subjected to the "three-bean-salad test." For the test, a styrene container, such as the Styrofoam ones found in delicatessens, and a polypropylene container were filled with a three-bean salad. The next day, a ring of liquid formed under the styrene container but not under the polypropylene one. This proved that the chemical structure of styrene provided a less effective oil barrier than that of polypropylene.

Formed-polypropylene containers also provided better clarity and better resistance to acids. A gas-barrier film, such as Saran or Eval, was added to polypropylene in a coextrusion (of a sandwich of films), providing extra shelf life for food packaging. If plastic containers with these barriers are aseptically retorted (sterilized with its contents to eliminate bacteria), shelf life could be extended without refrigeration or freezing. The industry wanted these properties but had not found them in other plastics. If Bedford could manufacture a coextruded product with these qualities, it might explode the market.

Another positive aspect was that European technology was capable of manufacturing the tooling to form polypropylene. Bedford felt that the European packaging industry was more advanced than the United States. European companies developed machines to form and die-cut styrene and vinyl in one step. Bedford saw this technology as the future of packaging in the United States if the machines could be adapted to polypropylene.

The Bedford team set out to study European polypropylene pressure-forming technology in 1977. A group of managers and engineers traveled to Europe to investigate the technology firsthand. During the trip, the men visited six leading machinery manufacturers. Bedford selected four of the manufacturers and placed orders of $10,000 each for samples of polypropylene bowls. It had the opportunity to visit three operating factories involved in high-speed-pressure formation. This was no small task considering that Europeans were not eager to give details of their manufacturing facilities and processes.

In one instance, Tom Haddock met with a German company from which Bedford had considered buying tooling. A couple of men from Holland were there looking at the tooling as well. Tom knew they had an SPPF (solid-phase-pressure-forming) operation and were ahead of Bedford technologically. The men were suspicious of Tom, concerned he might encroach on their technology. But Haddock did not let on to why he was there. He just explained that he was involved in a twist-tie manufacturing company in the United States.

At dinner, one of the men asked Tom whether he could dance with Barb, Tom's wife.

Tom replied, "Why don't you ask her?"

Barb accepted the offer, gaining the trust of the Hollanders, who allowed Tom to visit their manufacturing facility. The impressive operation was producing 50 million beer trays annually, holding 24 beers apiece. The enormous factory was way ahead of anything in United States—fully automated with operations handled by four or five employees. The visit, a stroke of luck, gave Haddock ideas of how he wanted Bedford to operate and what the future might hold.

"It was hard to admit that Europe was so far ahead of us," Haddock explained. "You are brought up to believe that if it is not made in the United States, it just is not made at all." It was amazing to him that small European countries like Holland were manufacturing high-tech products impossible then in the United States.

After the visit, Bedford Industries considered which manufacturer was the leader in the rapidly changing field of pressure-formation, settling on Maschinenbau Gabler GmbH of West Germany. Bedford thought this company would work best in the United States market. Bedford placed an order for pressure-forming equipment because Gabler cooperated in working with Bedford to adapt machinery for polypropylene.

Anticipating the arrival of the thermoforming equipment even as it advanced in twist-tie technology, Bedford was running short on space once again. The building that Bob Ludlow thought would never be filled had to double in size. To accommodate its growth, the company added 34,500 square feet to its warehouse.

Bedford Industries updated its classic B to a new 3-D version.

Aside from its thermoforming endeavors, the core of the company—the twist-tie product line—was taking over the industry. With the accomplishments and innovations of its first 12 years, Bedford Industries moved from its position as one of the three smallest twist-tie manufacturers to being a leader in the field. The proof? Its respected product and, in 1978, the fact that Plas-Ties sold its twist-tie manufacturing line to Bedford. Plas-Ties had been an industry leader a few years before—now it could no longer keep up with Bedford's innovation. Plas-Ties sold only its twist-tie line, continuing its manufacture of desktop twist-tie application machines and buying twist ties from Bedford for distribution. But the purchase expanded Bedford's market to include California, Nevada, and Arizona.

The twist-tie market was slowly maturing and becoming static. Bedford management felt that the company might not continue its large strides forward in that field. Future growth would parallel only the overall growth in population if the company gained no new product niches. Internationally, export tie markets had grown to about 8 or 9 percent of total sales, leveling off over the previous four years.

By 1979, the twist tie was no longer a new product but an everyday, household item. An article published in Consolidated Aluminum's journal, *Reflections*, made this clear. Following is a condensed version:

> Tiny Tools That Have a Million Uses:
> Which Is Why There Never Seem to Be Enough
> around the House
>
> Not so very long ago they didn't exist. Today they're practically everywhere, practically indispensable, and—like paperclips and pencils and other essentials of the modern home—capable of disappearing mysteriously just when they're needed most.
>
> And though almost everybody uses them, almost nobody knows what they're called.
>
> "Sure, I know what that is," people say with a smile when they're shown one. "It's a—it's one of those little wire things for keeping trash bags closed . . ."
>
> And, yes, "those little wire things for keeping trash bags closed."
>
> Bedford Industries calls them "twist ties," and Bedford Industries should know. The Worthington, Minnesota-based company has been manufacturing the little whatsits for 11 years now, and business seems to just keep getting better all the time . . .
>
> Bedford has become a supplier of twist ties to most of the major plastic-bag producers in the United States. In doing so, the company has won entry to millions of homes.
>
> It is the rapidly spreading domestic use of plastic bags, and the inclusion of ties in almost every package of bags sold, that has made the aluminum twist tie a standard mini-tool in homes across the country. This phenomenon has been accelerated by laws in ever-increasing numbers of communities requiring the replacement of old-fashioned crash-bang trash

cans with clean, quiet (and tightly, tidily closed) plastic bags.

The fact that most consumers get their supplies of twist ties solely through the purchase of plastic bags accounts in large part for an increasingly common household frustration: the disappearance of the ties long before all the accompanying bags are ready for fastening . . .

So we'll close with a simple but heartfelt expression of thanks to all the plastic-bag manufacturers who are thoughtful enough to put a few more twist ties than the absolutely required minimum in the packages of bags they sell.

They're helping us get it together!

One segment of the twist-tie industry ripe for growth was the production of tie-application machinery. The Burford Corporation had been the longtime leader, manufacturing equipment to automatically apply twist ties to bread bags in the bakery line.

Comedian Jonathan Winters pointed out the advantages of twist-tied plastic bags in a TV commercial.

Plas-Ties manufactured a small, desktop model, used for applying twist ties to items like candy bags. Doboy made a similar machine, which Bedford occasionally ordered. If Bedford had such a machine to sell, it would receive more twist-tie orders with every one it sold.

After careful consideration, the company decided not to enter the machinery business. Burford had the market cornered on bakery-tie equipment, and Plas-Ties had the dominant market share on small desktop machines. Bedford contemplated the purchase of Doboy's line, but its machines had many problems. Further, Burford and Plas-Ties recommended Bedford twist tie with every machine it sold. If Bedford manufactured competing machines, both companies might refrain from recommending Bedford twist tie. The company decided to retain its focus on the twist tie, while driving forward its newfound plastic-container niche.

5

Focus

T he next few years were stressful for Bedford Industries as it managed itself on two fronts. And as Bedford dove deeper into thermoforming technology, it began to get in over its head. The new market and new technology were difficult, requiring trial and error. Employees worked hard but did not see the fruits of their labor in the near term. And Bedford found itself in the midst of battle on the East Coast as "twist-tie wars" rocked the baking industry.

One offer brought Bedford new insight into the thermo- forming business. St. Regis Paper Company wanted to sell its candy-tray line to Bedford Industries. It vacuum-formed the brown-ribbed trays used for packaging cookies and chocolates— providing high profit margins. Bedford purchased the HDPE (high-density polyethylene) tray-forming equipment after St. Regis's third offer. It purchased the full sheeting line, including a Prodex extruder, six tray-forming machines, and dies.

Bedford learned to convert and extrude HDPE under production conditions. It mastered the extrusion process to

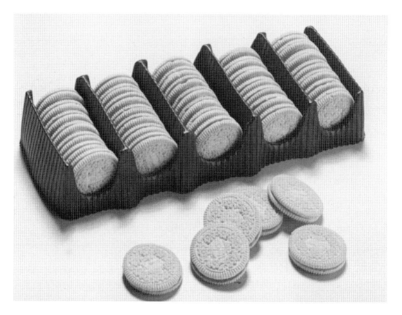

*Bedford took its first steps into the thermoforming industry
with Polytrays in 1979.*

accommodate close tolerances in temperature, water-cooling
molds, and tool-forming and trimming methods. But though they
learned a lot in the process, Haddock and Ludlow later agreed it
was not the best purchase for Bedford.

Bedford faced a dilemma with its new tray-forming line. Although the product had a good profit margin, the company could
produce only a small quantity per day because the machines were
small.

"You work all day to have $500 of product at the end. Well,
that's not worth anything," Ludlow explained. He wanted to find
a high-volume, low-margin product for Bedford. "With a high-
volume, tight-margin product, you have $500 to $1,000 sitting
there every half hour. You have $50,000 sitting there at the end
of the day, compared to $500 on a low-volume, high-margin
product—that's a big difference."

Many of Bedford's wire suppliers were overseas, which affected the company negatively as a series of strikes affected the industry. Bedford wanted to resolve the problem and simultaneously increase profit margins. In 1980, the company began drawing its own steel wire, making Bedford more self-sufficient. The old hatchery building was dedicated to wire production.

Terry Langland and Keith Fisher remember the problems Bedford confronted in trying to make wire. The process of wire drawing involved pulling steel rods through a series of dies until it was forced into the correct wire gauge. Requiring many dies to persuade the wire to come out correctly, it was not an easy task.

Wire drawing demanded a big pit filled with a drawing solution for wire pass-through. The pit eventually filled with sludge—a combination of drawing solution, steel, grease, and dirt. Finally, the Environmental Protection Agency told Bedford to clean the pit.

Bedford installed wire-drawing equipment
in the old hatchery building in 1980.

"That was the fun part, when you had to clean the sludge out," Langland recalled. "Never lucky enough to get that, but I hear it was pretty nasty-smelling."

A consultant came in for a few weeks to find a way to dispose of the sludge. Uncovering no other options, Bedford placed it in 55-gallon barrels and found a recycling company willing to take it away—for an exorbitant fee.

Meanwhile, Bedford waited for the Gabler pressure-forming equipment it had ordered from West Germany. It was still being assembled—by this time long overdue. Several other companies involved in the research of thermoformation equipment dropped out because the market for polypropylene packaging had changed in four years. Industry media had created a lot of hype surrounding the technology. Plastic companies saw the hype and increased the price for a plastic that had once been given little attention—polypropylene. Fearing the loss of the industry, injection molders had developed thin-wall technology in their molding capabilities and dropped prices—taking away an advantage of SPPF (solid-phase-pressure-forming). With its market advantage gone by 1981, Bedford remained the only company with European thermoformation machines still on order.

Bedford Plastics was incorporated as a wholly owned subsidiary of Bedford Industries in 1981. After the long wait and market turn, Bedford Plastics took delivery of the Gabler FP-700 deep-draw polypropylene pressure-forming equipment. It could produce more than 150 containers per minute and 50 million containers in one year. Two smaller Gabler Tima D450s thermoformers arrived later in the year, to produce lids via the SPPF process. To balance the annual output of the FP-700, two D450s were required. These were capable of producing more than 100 lids per minute and 25 million lids in a year.

Arriving at the loading dock, Bedford employees met a machine bent in half. During transit from Europe the machines supposedly had been dropped onto a shipyard dock. The Bedford engineers worked with cutting torches and welders to repair and modify the equipment in a long and difficult process to get it up and running. Doyle Moore explained that when the mold ran fine, the stacker did not work. When that was fixed, the sheet did not feed through the chains right. When that was corrected, the cooling and air pressure were not adequate. When that was fixed, a cutting edge somehow broke. The process seemed never-ending, but the employees continued to work. With a lot of determination, they finally began running the Gabler machines.

By 1982, Bedford had to expand its facility to accommodate the machinery that Bedford Plastics was acquiring. Construction began on a 9,600-square-foot research and development area for pressure-formation technology. The addition was finished just in

Bedford expanded its facility on Rowe Avenue by 9,600 square feet to house the growing Bedford Plastics operation, 1982.

time for Bedford Plastics to introduce its SPPF line. But there was no commercial market for the line—it had dried up in the past year. Bedford was able to land only Lever Brothers, Inc., in New Jersey. And Lever Brothers did not want a better margarine tub—but only a cheaper price. The account did not last long.

Kim Milbrandt, Bob Ludlow's son-in-law, joined the staff at Bedford Industries in 1982 as a manager in product development and marketing.

"I walked into a meeting with Bob Ludlow, Bob Boushek, and Ted Ludlow, and I recommended that we sell off the equipment as fast as possible. I couldn't see us ever making a go of it," Kim said. "It was an extremely difficult adventure because of the overhead for the new equipment and no market."

Even with media coverage, including a cover article in *Packaging Digest*, the company had trouble finding customers interested in the new packaging technology. "It seemed that polypropylene margarine tubs were not the better mouse trap," Milbrandt said.

After investing a lot of money in Bedford Plastics, the company questioned its decision. But the team chose to keep the thermoformation equipment and search for ways to use it.

The industry magazine, *Packaging Digest*, published an article about Bedford's investment in SPPF technology. "Bedford Bets Big on SPPF" provided an in-depth explanation of the machinery and process Bedford used in the production of bowls and lids (see appendix for complete article).

Bedford finally landed a big one—printing bowls for Land O' Lakes. The bowls were injection-molded by another manufacturer, and Bedford Plastics had a contract to print the dairy company's logo on the bowls. Bedford employees questioned the feel of the containers during printing. The bowls were slippery, as if the injection-molding firm had not correctly applied an antislip agent.

A week later, Land O' Lakes filled them, and the margarine later turned blue. Ink rubbed off on the inside of the nested bowls during shipment. As Bedford employees had suspected, the antislip agent had been incorrectly applied. Land O' Lakes did not catch the problem during filling, resulting in a recall and a potential lawsuit. The issue was settled out of court.

Disappointment continued when Bedford Plastics tried to land an account with General Mills, Inc., on a Care Bears™ project. Unrelated to food packaging, General Mills wanted Care Bears™ printed on deep-draw 12-inch plastic containers with rounded lids. But the opportunity fell through as the market for Care Bears™ died. The disappearance of the Land O' Lakes and Care Bears™ opportunities were heavy blows.

SPPF bowls, redesigned for the deli market, 1982.

Taking one more chance in 1982, Bedford redesigned its tooling for the growing deli market. "We looked at what packaging existed and saw a consistency in deli containers—they were all in styrene," Milbrandt said. Bedford Plastics knew it could create a better carry-out single-serving container than the styrene containers available. The company waited more than eight months for the new tooling from Germany since no firms in the United States made tooling that worked in the Gabler equipment.

During this time of change in the plastic-container industry, Bedford Industries saw growth in new twist-tie markets. The use

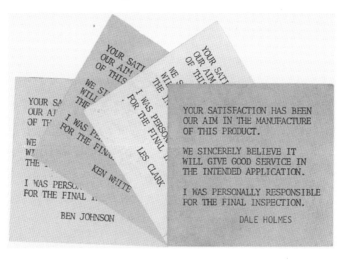

Quality control is a high priority at Bedford Industries. Supervisors such as Dale Holmes, Les Clark, Ken White, Ben Johnson, and Dale Greeley personally checked the quality of each twist-tie run, 1982.

of double-wire ties for closing paper cookie bags grew in 1982 when Frito-Lay, Inc., entered the cookie market. Bedford hoped for a stronger market with Frito-Lay putting competitive pressure on other cookie producers to add a reclosable feature.

Researching the concept for retail twist-tie packages, Bedford used focus groups to test market acceptance. The results of its 1983 market research prodded Bedford to introduce a line of consumer twist ties in cut lengths and on small spools. It was directed toward the home, shop, and garden markets. Bedford's flyer read:

> Twist 'N Tie plastic ties are colorfully packaged to sell on sight. Hang 'em up on J-Hooks, or stack 'em on a shelf. Your customers will come back again and again to buy these useful ties for home, shop and garden. The more you use 'em, the more uses you can find for Twist 'N Tie. They're durable and reusable. Perfect for sealing, securing, hanging and storing household items; securing tomato plants, flowers, shrubs, etc. You name it!

In summer 1983, Bob Lauro saw an ad in a Connecticut newspaper by a company looking for a sales representative. He answered the ad, placed by Bedford Industries. He interviewed with Bob Boushek and Bob Gantzer, the sales manager, at the Holiday Inn in Hartford. It was a long process, but Gantzer returned for a follow-up interview, taking Lauro on as the regional salesman. Lauro started in October with the region of New England—extending south to Philadelphia and east to Buffalo.

When Lauro started, one-third of Bedford's sales were with three major accounts. The big three included Nabisco with cookies, Mobil with Hefty garbage bags, and Union Carbide with GLAD® bags. Aside from the Bedford Plastics endeavor, Bedford had not diversified much beyond its bakery and garbage-bag industries.

Lauro focused on bakeries on the East Coast. The region had several major twist-tie competitors, including Alcar, Tite Ties, and Package Containers.

"The name of the game was attack your competitors," Lauro said. But it became more than an attack—it was an all-out twist-tie war. A competitor called on Bedford customers and reduced the price, prompting at least one bakery to switch the brand of twist ties it used. Lauro went back into that bakery (and every other bakery) every other week to hold onto customers, generally reclaiming them with Bedford service and its popular spool adapter. The bakery market—the backbone of the company—was crucial to Bedford.

Competing companies made the East Coast a difficult market. When Bud Witten, the owner of Tite Ties, died, a group from the bakery industry bought his twist-tie manufacturing equipment. The group formed a company called Middletown Packaging and kept Lauro working hard to retain Bedford's customers. Because it came from inside the baking industry, the new company had the right connections. A few years later, Middletown was sold to Bettendorf Stanford, Inc., in Salem, Illinois. Developing a product line much like Bedford's, including a double-wire tie, Bettendorf Stanford posed a strong competitive threat. It resulted in one of Lauro's most fierce twist-tie wars, and a struggle to keep Bedford products in the bakeries.

Bedford's superior product and better service prevailed. It continued to pick off bakeries one by one, and by 1989, the company controlled almost the entire East Coast market.

6

Compete

Oh, you're the company with the yellow boxes!" was a frequent comment to Bedford Plastics employees and salesmen. Something as simple as a yellow box in place of a traditional brown one had a profound effect on public recognition. Bedford Plastics wanted its products to stand out in warehouses and grocery stores. Shipping personnel appreciated the yellow boxes because they easily spot them in warehouses. "The yellow box company" became a Bedford Plastics "trademark."

Bedford Plastics made a turnaround in the next two years. The company had made mistakes, learning invaluable knowledge from them. More important, Bedford had not been afraid to fail. The company set sail in uncharted waters and weathered the storm to find dry land ahead. The risks taken and the grueling learning process began to pay off.

In 1983 as Bedford Plastics awaited the arrival of new deli tooling from Germany, it prepared to take on the deli market full force. Jim Hill, an experienced plastic-bowl marketer, was hired in 1984 to sell the clear polypropylene containers. Having worked in the deli business for years, he held many key contacts and promised large sales.

The deli tooling finally arrived, but the German company had packed the equipment incorrectly—and it shattered. The broken tools were sent back, and Bedford Plastics was delayed again for six months. Bedford used the time wisely, learning to de-nest and obtain a better bowl shape. After the tools arrived and Bedford began manufacturing again, it printed deli containers with better clarity and greater resistance than other containers on the market. The product was ready for the challenge of rigorous food requirements, those of such foods as peanut butter, Mexican salsa, cheese, and three-bean salad.

Jim Hill came through with his promise—within six months Bedford went from no sales to an overwhelming number of orders in the spring of 1984.

"Things quickly began to happen," Milbrandt said. "The yellow deli boxes gradually filled up the aisles in Bedford's warehouse." The polypropylene deli container outperformed the styrene one-time-use containers.

"The deli business is basically what got us going," Milbrandt said, "but our product still lacked the special attributes that were needed to get the big sales." The industry needed more than printing and improved resistance and clarity to switch to Bedford's containers.

Bedford employees often took the bowls and lids home to use in their kitchens. Many of them tried using the plastic bowls in their microwaves—and it worked. Engineers and resin suppliers warned that the bowls could not withstand the microwave, but Bedford Plastics thought that microwavability might set its bowls above the rest. Against the odds, Bedford Plastics sent the polypropylene containers for testing at Litton Industries' Microwave Division and at Cornell University. The testing, approved by Gertrude Armbrusten, lead food-packaging specialist at Cornell, came back positive. Bedford had found its niche— microwavable plastic bowls.

Bedford Plastics was one of the first companies to use the "triple wave" symbol, with its new Microlite logo. In the mid-1980s it became the in- dustry standard for identifying microwavable products.

Bedford Plastics began gearing up to introduce its line of microwavable and freezable food containers. It trademarked the name Microlite for the new product line. This name, later regis- tered, became the industry standard.

The company organized a focus group in Minneapolis to review the product and provide a marketing strategy. Bedford management wanted empirical evidence for the potential of Microlite® bowls as "indestructible Tupperware substitutes." The focus group's response was discouraging. After six weeks it came back with few positive things to say for Microlite® bowls. Its members were frustrated because the bowls deformed after a few uses and certain foods stained them. The bowls were not inde- structible, as Bedford had promised.

The company was ready to give up on Microlite®, but Bob Ludlow suggested another try, and another focus group was as- sembled in Minneapolis. This time Bedford presented the bowls as disposable and economical. The new focus group came back six weeks later raving about the bowls. Rather than expecting the bowls to be indestructible cookware, the members saw them as an item to be thrown away. The group was excited to get multiple uses from each bowl. "We learned a lot, and that probably saved us from creating a major marketing disaster. What if we had started without those focus groups in promoting Bedford's products?" Milbrandt asked. Bedford Plastics no longer had a styrene replacement but a product with unique features and a lower price.

Bedford Plastics aimed its first marketing strategy at retail mass merchandisers. Bedford landed Target stores, but the product was not brought to full-retail level—and there was not enough sales turnover in the first six months. Bedford advertised to the public through Sunday newspapers and TV inserts. Microlite®

"The swoosh lady" was not using hotpads in this picture on a bag of bowls, 1983.

products also appeared in catalogs such as those of Hanover House and Miles Kimball. The production floor was finally busy, generating high sales as the result of such opportunities.

One day, Kim Milbrandt received a call from an elderly woman in Florida and her attorney. The attorney wanted to sue Bedford because the woman had burned her hands while taking a bowl from the microwave. Milbrandt was confused—the bags were printed with diagrams and a warning insert that consumers must use hot pads to remove the bowls from the microwave. She explained that she saw Bedford's advertisement with "the swoosh lady" moving a bowl from the freezer to the microwave. What Bedford did not realize was that "the swoosh lady" was shown without hot pads. Milbrandt was quick to apologize and thank her for pointing out the mistake. He explained that they would correct the error and that she had probably saved others from getting burned. He offered to settle by providing a lifetime supply of plastic bowls.

The woman's attorney wanted to follow through on litigation, but the woman did not care about the money—she wanted the plastic bowls. Bedford Plastics destroyed about 50,000 misprinted bags and printed new bags with "the swoosh lady" using hot pads. Bedford sent the woman a large box of every bowl size, asking her to call whenever she needed more.

As it outgrew the 9,600-square-foot research and development addition, Bedford Plastics realized it needed its own production facility. Customers were asking when the company could be in full-scale production, but it did not have the space or equipment to accomplish that. Bedford Plastics needed a larger building for new machinery and the proper flow of manufacturing material. It found the right facility, a 67,000-square-foot factory in Sioux Falls, just an hour from Worthington.

In announcing the move, Bedford emphasized that there would be no loss of jobs in Worthington. "It was the immediate need for warehouse and manufacturing space," Bob Ludlow said. A few employees with management and operational experience moved to Sioux Falls with the expansion.

Bedford Plastics facility in Sioux Falls, 1984.

The move went quickly—three months after the purchase of the Sioux Falls building in 1984, it was completely remodeled, and Bedford moved in.

"I remember walking with some men from Campbell Soup's New Jersey headquarters through the newly purchased and still empty Sioux Falls building," Milbrandt said. "One of them stated that it would easily take their crews more than a year to convert this plant into a useful production facility—that was two months before we moved in."

The speed and hard work that Bedford employees put into converting the Sioux Falls site astounded Bedford *and* Campbell Soup Company. "The move went well physically," Milbrandt explained. "The difficulty was more a mental and emotional one. Seventeen people relocated with the move and began to build another team, like the superb one in Worthington. The distance and the inexperienced workforce made it difficult to work out the bugs for all involved, from engineering through administration. But again, Bedford's camaraderie and tenacity allowed it to achieve levels that other companies only dream of."

Bedford Plastics was almost totally independent of the plant in Worthington. It had its own sales, engineering, and maintenance departments. But duplication proved expensive. The company shared some members of the engineering staff and the accounting department, but otherwise Bedford Plastics' decisions were separate.

In the mid-1980s, changes in America's eating habits caused the microwave market to explode. Suddenly, Bedford Plastics microwave packaging took off. Bedford was the only American manufacturer with a microwavable tray, which created large demand for its product. The company went from no production to skyrocketing sales in less than three years.

Bedford then pursued the step beyond microwavable containers—"ovenable" containers. Engineers worked closely with Goodyear Tire and Rubber Company, Eastman Kodak Company, and Campbell Soup to find a resin that holds up in the microwave and oven. They found CPET (crystallized polyethylene terephthalate)—the next breakthrough Bedford hoped for.

Manufacturing CPET containers was not easy, as it allowed only a narrow margin of error in the production process. The temperature of the plastic had to remain within one or two degrees of optimum for the bowls to form correctly. But by 1985, the Bedford team prevailed, bringing CPET trays and containers into full, commercial production.

"One of the biggest events that rocked the nation was our invention of the plastic TV-dinner tray with Campbell Soup,"

Boushek said. Ovenable bowls and containers were a new concept internationally. Containers that could be used in the oven or microwave were the perfect packaging solution for the world's growing on-the-go eating habits.

The Swanson TV-dinner tray could be heated in both oven and microwave, 1985.

In 1985, Bedford Plastics qualified to manufacture Campbell Soup Company's Swanson's TV-dinner trays. Packaging magazines constantly published complimentary articles about Campbell Soup for its innovative packaging. As Campbell Soup's supplier of CPET trays, Bedford Plastics received a lot of press. Other manufacturing firms followed, but they found it difficult to compete with Bedford.

Bedford gained a reputation for making stress-free, polypropylene plastic. Campbell Soup used Bedford Plastics as its testing facility for new CPET resins. Rampart, a division of Shell Corporation, requested that Bedford Plastics make polypropylene sheet for use in prototype pressure forming in Europe. Bedford Plastics was on the cutting edge of plastic-extrusion technology, and it was becoming one the world's largest plastic-container manufacturers. Goodyear, the company that manufac-tured the granular CPET resin, reported that Bedford alone con-sumed 15 percent of its production.

The quality of the Bedford Plastics container generated a lot of attention. Deep draw (longest in the world), high clarity, and uniformity of wall thickness were its most impressive features. German machinery manufacturers and resin suppliers demanded Bedford containers for displays at European plastics expositions. CPET trays attracted attention as "the latest in packaging tech-nology" at international conventions.

Bedford Plastics gained accounts from a variety of large food processors. Campbell Soup Company worked a long time and spent millions to develop a microwavable meal including a sand-wich and soup in a bowl supplied by Bedford. Research indicated the product was a winner, and Campbell advertised on TV during the 1985 Super Bowl. Then two young Campbell MBAs decided to conduct just one more market test—in San Diego in summer—before its release. The Souper Combo was not popular there, and Campbell decided to drop the combo and, with it, the specially developed Bedford bowls. But Bedford developed more innova-tive packaging for other customers—Swanson's TV-dinner trays, Hormel's Top Shelf domes, Pepperidge Farm's Petite Croissant trays, Pillsbury Brownie Mix trays, and General Mills Hamburger Helper trays—who kept the sales force busy. Many smaller cus-tomers purchased Bedford containers as well.

Sales rolled in more quickly than production could accom-modate. Each year, Bedford purchased new machinery and added forming stations to keep up. Through 1986 and 1987, the com-pany purchased pressure-forming and coextrusion machines that included Armacs, Thermtrols, and Gablers. The new machinery, along with new resins and resin combinations formed through coextrusion, provided versatility and flexibility for creating new container shapes and solving packaging problems for which there had been no solutions just a few years earlier.

In just eight years Bedford Plastics grew from a startup into a business with almost $20 million in sales and 200 employees, working around the clock seven days a week.

7

Celebrate

On August 24, 1985, Dale Holmes and Mike Hamman made a late-night coffee stop at the Worthington Perkins around 2 A.M. A police officer in a booth next to them received a call on the police scanner. Another police officer on the highway a few blocks from Bedford had seen flames. Bedford Industries was on fire! Holmes and Hamman jumped into Holmes's El Camino and followed the police cars and fire trucks to the factory. As two of the first people on the scene, they could see the flames from blocks away and as high as the building. Bob Ludlow was quickly at the scene, as well as John Van Ede, awakened by a phone call from Patricia Ludlow. "I got my clothes on and ran down there," Van Ede recalled. "I couldn't believe it!"

The fire was contained to the back of a dump truck from the local landfill. But it had started burning through the roof and into the building. Little damage was done thanks to the fast action of employees and of the fire and police departments. The fire did not shut Bedford down, but it was one of the closest calls Bedford had faced. The cause was never determined with certainty, but authorities believe a cigarette started it. If the fire had burned longer undiscovered, it might have been disastrous to Bedford and its employees.

The year 1986 marked the 20-year anniversary for Bedford, which held a companywide celebration at Pioneer Village and the Nobles County Fairgrounds. An article in the *Worthington Daily Globe* gave a taste of Bedford's 20-year history.

Bedford especially celebrated how widespread its products had become. Bob Ludlow remarked on how surprised he was one day when he went to a local grocery store to find Bedford products everywhere. He saw twist ties on cookies, crackers, breads, garbage bags, diapers, and frozen-food products. He found plastic containers in the deli, candy aisle, and meat department. He said that the next time someone asked him what Bedford made, he would take them to a grocery store.

The charred loading dock on the day after the fire, 1985.

The Worthington Daily Globe noted Bedford's 20th anniversary with the photo above and this caption: "Twist ties for breadwrappers, garbage bags and cracker containers—and dozens of other uses—are manufactured at Bedford Industries, Inc., in Worthington in a variety of colors. Bob Ludlow, sitting in the warehouse division of the plant, founded Bedford Industries 20 years ago. He said he entered the food-packaging industry at a time when it happened to be expanding in that direction. The company now also makes trays for convenience goods." (Randy Lindemann photo)

As Bedford celebrated 20 years of corporate success, it was often recognized in the packaging industry for its outstanding products. As president of the firm, Bob Ludlow was commended for his leadership ability and asked to write an article for the June 1987 edition of *Small Business Report*. His article, "Promoting Ethical Business Practices," in part:

> A primary responsibility of the president or CEO is to create and promote a corporate culture that is committed to ethical business practices. It is impossible to have an ethical company, I believe, when this goal is not championed by a top executive.

Employees are made aware of a company's commitment to ethical business practices through the firm's written objectives and its policies and procedures. However, written statements are meaningless unless this commitment is demonstrated in the daily management style of top and senior management . . .

I feel that the president has the moral responsibility to be concerned about the effects that business decisions will have on employees' economic security. When evaluating major decisions, top management too often is primarily concerned with how an action will affect its own financial security. But decisions should also be evaluated in terms of what is best for employees. The more ethical the company is in its treatment of employees, the more committed employees will be to the firm.

Bob Ludlow's managing style was unique. He did not like meetings, and he avoided them unless they involved a big project or a lot of money. His version of a meeting was to walk through Bedford, talking to people individually to see what was happening. He made a tour through the plant every day to check on projects and visit with employees. In Tom Haddock's opinion, this made for a stress-free environment, even though Ludlow often appeared at the wrong moment.

Dale Holmes ran a twist-tie line, and Ludlow often stopped to see how things were going. "Inevitably, whenever he would stop by, we would have a wire out, paper tear, or something would go wrong," Holmes said.

One day, Ludlow told him, "You know, Dale, I'm going to stop coming to see you because every time I come, everything goes wrong."

John Van Ede had a similar experience when Ludlow gave a tour of the original factory to a couple of bankers. Ludlow showed the bankers the line that Van Ede was running. As they stood by the machine, a gear flew out and hit the wall. Ludlow and the bankers looked at each other and quickly walked out.

Bedford Plastics had some hard questions to answer in 1987. Amoco Foam Products Company, a subsidiary of Amoco Corporation, approached Bedford about buying its plastics division. At first, Bedford management refused, but the offers continued. Finally, Amoco gave two options: Bedford could sell or Amoco would enter the market as competition.

There was no easy answer. The division could not stop Amoco from entering the industry, and the corporate conglomerate could easily afford the best in equipment. The name Amoco alone would give it immediate sales and take from Bedford's market share. The offer appealed to the future Bedford Industries, which looked strained by the debt acquired with Bedford Plastics. Even though Bedford's market research predicted a bright future for the plastic-container industry, the future of the division was uncertain—especially if Amoco Foam chose to enter the market.

Bedford management made a difficult decision. Bearing in mind the long-term security of employees, Bedford Industries considered it best to sell Bedford Plastics to Amoco Foam. The process involved took six months of price negotiations and another three months of human-relations negotiation to close the deal. One requirement from Bedford was that Amoco stay in Sioux Falls and not let any employees go. In 1988, the deal closed, and Amoco Foam Products Company started a new division named Amoco High Performance Packaging.

The timing was a stroke of luck for Bedford—two years later the packaging market declined dramatically. One of Bedford's largest customers, Campbell Soup, discontinued 256 products that used bowls and trays. Bedford Plastics had been sold to

Amoco right at the industry's peak. The market research that predicted continued growth was wrong.

The explanation for the market decline lay in the need of retail and commercial industries for more shelf space. Bags replaced rigid, plastic packaging and square boxes replaced round bowls. Bedford was fortunate to leave the industry at its peak.

"I think Bob Ludlow was way ahead of his time," Boushek reflected. "I don't think the world was ready for him yet. I think he saw something that was there, but the world was not ready to do it."

Bedford Plastics was a true start-up and a success story. Making it work was not easy, and the company had its fair share of troubles in its youth. But because of dedicated employees and company tenacity, Bedford played a role in revolutionizing the microwavable and dual-ovenable packaging industries.

III

Reinvention

8

Invest, deliver, expand, and grow

B edford Industries occasionally received ideas for new products from individuals outside the company. This handwritten letter laid out one idea of an 11-year-old boy who had toured a bakery with his class:

> Dear Sirs, I have written to your company because I have a very good idea. It's not just for me, but for all the buyers of your product (your bread). Here is my idea, instead of using those old twist ties that you always lose, you can mold the wire that the twist ties are made of into the bag that the bread is in, so you just twist the bag and it's done, and there's not little twist ties to lose. If you like my idea, I just want to know, I'm not being greedy, but how much would you pay me for this idea? Please write back as soon as possible. Bye for now.

Bedford had considered the idea in the past but found it impossible to make such an item. Collaboration between bag manufacturers and twist-tie manufacturers was difficult. Gluing a tie to a bag and designing machines to make the process work was expensive. From the perspective of the bakery, its tying process already worked and there was little incentive to change it.

Bedford Industries was again searching for new ideas. Although it had operated independent of Bedford Plastics, the plastic division's sale to Amoco was a major change for the company as a whole. The focus of the entire organization now returned to the twist tie. The attention and excitement centering on the blooming plastics division was gone. Once again, Bedford set out to find new markets and product ideas for the twist tie.

The core twist-tie product was a solid commodity, making up 91 percent of Bedford's total sales. Most startling was the volume of twist tie sold (see page 161 for more data): By the 20th anniversary of Bedford Industries (1966 to 1986) the company made an estimated 56 billion feet of tie, around 11 million miles—equivalent to 426 trips around the earth or 22 trips to the moon and back. In 1988 alone, more than 6 billion feet of tie was manufactured—almost 24 million feet per day and 1.1 million miles during the year. That year Bedford made enough twist tie to encircle the earth 46 times or make 2.5 round trips to the moon. Simply stated, Bedford made a lot of twist tie!

Two of Bedford's new semi trucks, known as "B trucks," 1983.

Freight costs rose continually, putting a strain on Bedford's pricing. The solution lay in finding a less expensive way to transport goods. With a large investment, Bedford started its own trucking service. Not only did it reduce shipping costs, it also gave the company better control of the shipping process. A small truck was leased in 1980, with three semi trucks added in 1985. A 1988 *Tieline* (Bedford's company newsletter, which started in 1986) announced changes in Bedford's shipping program:

> Changes have been made to better serve the customer and Bedford Industries. It's called Bedford Transportation, Ltd. By becoming a completely independent company, with ICC authority, we are now able to add freight from other companies to our truckloads and can also backhaul other freight into the area. This will not only help to serve our customer better, it will also help to enable us to hold down the rising cost of freight. We have three very good drivers—Dick, Tom, and Doyle. With them on the job and a lot of help from Karla in accounting, we can look for a lot of good things to happen in trucking to help us all.

Following the renowned history for customer service, Bedford Transportation, Ltd., was founded in 1988. With each truck driving more than 120,000 miles a year, Bedford assembled a fleet of four trucks to provide better delivery to customers across the United States and Canada. The trucking division became one of Bedford's greatest assets for customer service. General manager Bob Boushek believed it was one of the company's milestones and one of its smartest decisions.

Bedford gave up on its wiredrawing effort in 1988, selling its equipment to Keystone. Attempts to manufacture cheaper and more consistent wire were not as successful as the team had hoped. Although the facility was making an average of 65,000 pounds of wire per month and as much as 120,000 pounds in a good month, it was cheaper to purchase wire overseas where the consistency was improving. Through the venture, Bedford learned a lot about wire tension and bearings, in the long run saving hundreds of dollars a month.

Bedford made a wide range of specialized ties, including one with a reflective material on one side. These ties found interesting uses, unanticipated by Bedford. For example, a company in Arkansas used the reflective ties as trail markers. The *Arkansas Democrat Gazette* ran an article about them on August 4, 1988:

> Twist Ties Mark Trail
> Ever get lost trying to find your favorite duck blind, deer stand or turkey-hunting spot in the big woods?
> There are many ways to mark a trail. But in order for your markers to be useful before daylight and after dark, fluorescent material or paint is required.
> An extraordinarily simple method has been developed by a Cabot resident.
> "Limblights" are fluorescent, reflective trail markers that appear to be nothing more than the same twist-tie strips found keeping plastic bags closed in every American household.
> All a person has to do is shine a flashlight to spot the trail markers, which can be twisted around limbs or tacked onto tree trunks.
> Around the house, they can be used to mark a safe route of escape in case of fire or to guide a sleepy child to the bathroom.
> Attached to an important key on a key chain, they can make selection easy.
> You may soon be finding "Limblights" in the Wal-Mart stores. Representatives of Ben Pearson Archery of Pine Bluff reportedly have expressed interest in using the little devices for bow-hunting.

Bedford Industries projected its largest year ever for 1988. The efforts of engineering, maintenance, and production people allowed Bedford to tackle some difficult projects. For instance, large trash-bag manufacturers automated packaging lines, prompting the use of gang ties on auto-feed machinery. Bedford also developed a double-wire gang tie for a trash bag company in Canada, though it almost abandoned the project. "If it hadn't been for the efforts of the people on the production floor, we may have phased out that product," Ludlow said.

One reason for Bedford's success in product improvement and innovation was that many of the efforts came directly from people on the production floor. Ludlow explained, "Before we abandon a product line because of non-competitiveness, we always try to see if we can save on material and improve on machine efficiencies. We have done this in the past, but in the future we will always try to get direct input from the production floor. Quality and improved production efficiencies are what keep a product competitive. If quality slips and production efficiencies don't continually improve, a product is lost and business volume declines. Everyone's input is important."

After Bedford Plastics was sold, Bedford Industries retained its momentum. There was a push to keep developing ideas and evolving into markets. Bob Boushek remembered Ludlow coming to him and asking, "So, what do we do now?" Bedford's next few years took the form of grass-roots evolution, as opposed to the multimillion-dollar investment in European thermoformation technology during the Bedford Plastics years.

"What can we do with this scrap?" was a question commonly posed by the Bedford team. In 1988, Bedford faced increasing landfill prices, projected as high as $50,000 a year. This was a time when environmental issues were hot and landfill was not a secure asset. There were rumors of stringent regulations to be placed on discarded materials as well as on the quantities allowed. If these regulations caught Bedford off guard, the company might end up in a tough situation. Bedford wanted to maximize twist-tie by-products currently being thrown away. Some recycling efforts, such as bailing scrap for target stops at archery ranges, had been made, but it was not enough.

A member of the 4-H community came to Boushek, asking what Bedford Industries could do with all the plastic going to the dump. The Bedford team conducted considerable research into the recycling of industrial scrap and products that might be manufactured from it. The team intended to turn wasted trim from twist ties into salable products. Its focus became recycled lumber, a product recently launched by a few other companies but one that needed improvement. It was a product with advantages over traditional lumber, and it offered many opportunities.

Bob Hill had been in charge of human resources at Bedford Industries since 1979. When Bedford Plastics took off, Linda Hill (no relation to Bob) was hired to help in that department. After the sale of Bedford Plastics to Amoco, there was no need for two human resource directors. Bob Hill wanted a new challenge, particularly in sales and marketing, since he had been involved with marketing organizations in the past. Bob Ludlow gave Hill the opportunity to see what he could do with the recycled-plastic-lumber project over the next six months.

With Hill as supervisor, Bedford started a pilot line for manufacturing plastic lumber—using twist-tie trim and post-consumer polyethylene from milk and water bottles. Schapp's Salvage, the local sanitation company, was hired to collect milk jugs in the community. As Bedford's demand for raw material increased, Schapp's began to draw from outside of Worthington.

The plastic lumber Bedford developed had several advantages over traditional wood. The resin base of HDPE (high-density polyethylene) plastic did not crack or splinter. Bedford colored the plastic, leaving no need for paint or treatment. In the agricultural industry, the lumber was virtually indestructible around livestock. Animals did not chew on it, and it did not absorb moisture to promote bacteria growth. The only drawback of the "lumber" was that it bowed when exposed to varied temperatures. Despite that drawback, Bedford created a great new product, and the company was excited to see what it would do on the market.

On May 18, 1990, Hill and team announced that the plastic lumber was ready for sale. Offering the product only in black, Bedford sold it at manufacturing cost to get consumer feedback. After a positive reaction and a response to suggestions for improvement, Bedford Plastic Timbers® was ready for full manufacture and marketing. The Bedford team celebrated its first "big" order in 1991–$5,000 worth. That first order was only the beginning. During the first full year of 1991, Bedford manufactured enough planks to go to the moon and back—twice.

Bedford offered plastic lumber in many more colors and sizes. Customers found practical applications for the product, including tables, benches, parking stops, and signposts. Keith Fisher, later head of maintenance, constructed many of these items for trade shows and Bedford use. He found plastic lumber's durability and life expectancy a major advantage over traditional wood. For instance, his picnic table certainly was not a candidate for an easy steal or blowing over in the wind—it weighed in at 416 pounds. He also found that the lumber was slick on the snow. Fisher and other employees built a toboggan from it, nicknamed "Fear of God." At least one broken arm was to its "credit."

The February 14, 1992, edition of the *Tri-State Neighbor* featured Bedford Plastic Timbers®:

Bedford's Recycled Plastic Has Agricultural Uses
WORTHINGTON, MN–Agriculture is no stranger to recycling. For years, agriculture has made use of waste or low value products.

One of the newest recycled products used by farmers is recycled plastic. Bedford Industries of Worthington, MN, is producing plastic timbers made in part from scrap or waste from the twist tie manufacturing process . . .

"Farmers use their imagination for a number of applications." [Bob Hill] said ordinary hand tools could be used because the timbers saw, nail, and drill like wood.

Paul Hohensee, a Worthington area farmer, has used the timbers to construct a calf-feed bunk. "You want to be sure you are accurate, because once a nail is driven in, it is almost impossible to pull it out." He said the feed bunk is fairly heavy, so the calves don't move it around. "It doesn't seem to freeze down as easily as a wood bunk does . . . "

"The timbers are excellent to use in landscaping." Hill said the plastic timbers are being used by parks and recreation departments and in lawn and garden applications. "A number of park benches have been constructed."

Bedford Plastic Timbers® received national recognition from the National Environmental Council in Washington, D.C., for its efforts in recycling. And Bedford's program was listed in the "Environmental Success Index," for having a positive impact on the local landfill. During a five-month period, 100,000 pounds of waste, previously destined for the dump, was manufactured into plastic timber. The savings in landfill cost for five months was more than $10,000.

Bedford received grants from the State of Minnesota's Office of Waste Management to continue its recycling efforts. Still there were disbelievers. In May 1992, the Market Development Coordination Council reviewed grant applications and wrote: "Members were skeptical of the economic viability and marketability of plastic lumber." But because it was impressed by

Bedford's other markets and the company's success, the committee granted funds for the project.

In looking back, Bob Boushek remembered one unique idea
for plastic lumber that involved his neighbor, who worked in the
construction business. This neighbor was reshingling a house,
but the tar paper was blowing off. Boushek said, "All he had on
hand was tar paper, and he couldn't get beyond that. He had seen
some red double-wire .315 tie in my garage, so he came over and
asked if he could borrow a bunch." The contractor laid the twist-
tie down on the tar strips and stapled them so the tar paper could
not blow away. The Bedford team took the idea and created
Rolath®—a product made from recycled plastic for roofing.

Minnesota Technology, Winter 1993, published an article
featuring Bedford's diversification from the twist tie and empha-
sizing plastic lumber. An excerpt from the article shows Bob
Ludlow's caution in the industry:

> Despite the apparent promise of plastic lumber, Bob Ludlow
> is guarded in his projections for the product. "It's a tough
> business, waste recovery," he explains. "Several U.S. compa-
> nies are making recycled-plastic lumber, but more have gone
> broke than are in it today." He says customers tend to be con-
> servative in their purchases, wanting to test the lumber over
> the course of a couple of harsh winters and weighing its con-
> siderably greater cost against its advertised durability before
> buying the material in large quantities. "It could become a big
> part of our business, but we don't know how fast that market
> will develop. We have to be pretty cautious, because the do-
> mestic markets for recycled products are growing slowly."

Although Hill was in charge of plastic lumber, Ludlow
stepped in occasionally. In one instance, Bob Boushek received a
proposal for half-a-truckload of red lumber. Hill and Boushek
pursued the project, testing samples of red lumber. During the

early stages of the project, Ludlow did not think Bedford should chase it any further. Red fades quickly when left outside—making Bedford's lumber look like a poor product. But the lumber samples worked, and the order was made. Hill chuckled as he reflected on Ludlow's reaction the day the order came through. "He walked into my office and said, 'Hill, what part of *no* don't you understand?" After Hill explained that the project was for an indoor application, Ludlow was happy. But he recommended that Hill not make any more red.

During the next few years Bedford's recycled-plastic- lumber department grew quickly; the division became profitable by 1997. Hill believes the people made it work. Bedford's plastic lumber became successful in a market where many others failed.

9

Recycle and customize

Bob Ludlow was at a trade show on the West Coast when he came across Chinese-made metallic ribbon with wire in it. It was similar to the twist tie, but it was to be used for decorative purposes. Ludlow liked the decorative purpose and thought it was a product that Bedford could make better. In the spirit of the original driving force behind Bedford's success with its core twist-tie products, the Bedford team set out to pursue a new market, for using the twist tie in a new way.

The Chinese-made ribbon Ludlow found had been made with a process similar to twist-tie production, but with different paper. Bedford saw more decorative twist-tie products at the WF&FSA (Wholesale Florist & Florist Supply Association) show in Atlanta. Also, the company was getting requests for decorative products from the West Coast. Bedford decided there was a market for a twist tie of different materials—custom and designer products.

The first customer for a custom tie was Presentations Plus out of Minneapolis. Presentations Plus shipped screen-printed gift wrap to Bedford. Bedford ran wire into it for a final product to be used in retail-store displays and decorations. This double-wire tie marked the debut of a new line called Bedford Bendable Ribbon®. The first official order for the product went to R & J Wholesale Supply in Sioux Falls. R & J purchased 36 different styles of ribbon, totaling 2,700 feet.

The company hoped that Bedford Bendable Ribbon® might open a new sales avenue to counter decreasing sales in other areas. The traditionally stable trash-bag twist-tie market came under fire as bag producers looked for different ways to close trash bags. Mobil's Hefty line integrated handles into the garbage bag, bypassing the need for the tie. Mobil also wanted to eliminate the twist tie. Hefty advertised against the twist in television commercials with the jingle: "Hefty, Hefty Cinch Sak. Wimpy, wimpy, wimpy. Hefty . . ." The garbage-bag business never disappeared, but Bedford wanted to compensate for the decreasing market and develop another for future security.

Planning for growth in the decorative and custom industry, Bedford expanded its telemarketing and sales capabilities. Why did Bedford expand the sales department despite shrinking markets? Ludlow had a rationale: On average, a distributor of Bedford's cut ties bought from $5,000 to $10,000 worth per year. The sales force would have to pick up 80 to 150 new distributors to make up for Mobil, if Mobil phased out of the cut-tie market.

"It takes a lot of work, a lot of telephoning, and a lot of calls to pick up a hundred new customers," Ludlow remarked. "This means we will eventually have to have additional help in telemarketing and order-entry areas." Bedford expected the decorative and custom-tie ribbon sales to increase and wanted to plan for handling calls and service questions. As Lloyd Tinklenberg said, "If you don't plan for change and new products, you can plan to shut your doors in ten years."

The craft industry had potential because it was always looking for something new and exciting. Bedford needed an industry insider, and it found one in Cindy Groom-Harry, a craft designer and consultant from Iowa. She had a lot of ideas for Bedford Bendable Ribbon®, and she fired up Ludlow about the market. Boushek remembered Ludlow saying "We can do it" and Cindy Groom-Harry saying "We can sell it."

To accomplish Ludlow and Harry's goals, Bedford set up an in-house, direct retail program. The company worked its way into national chain stores, including 250 Ben Franklin stores, 160 Michael & Dupey stores, and 90 Lee Wards stores. Bedford Bendable Ribbon® took off quickly in the craft industry.

The floral market also had strong potential, with its demand for wired products for decorations. Bedford hired a floral consultant to oversee its floral markets. It might be difficult to attack

The Bedford Bendable Ribbon® show booth, 1990.

111

both craft and floral markets at the same time, but Bedford had done such a thing before and thought it could do it again.

The following articles, published nationwide, introduced Bedford's craft and floral products:

Bend Over Backwards

BEDFORD INDUSTRIES, INC. has gone the extra mile to provide your craft customers with a unique offering that will enhance their craft, seasonal, and jewelry projects. Bedford Bendable Ribbon® may be twisted, bent, curled, or bowed, obediently following the desires of the creator and remaining true forever. It is available in six metallic colors and six widths (from ¹⁄₁₆ to 2¾ inches) and is sold in kits, hanks, and rolls, which will be supported with a project sheet and book program. Plan-a-grams, sample boards, and other sales aids are available to the retailer.

—Creative Products News, August 1990

The Bedford Twist

Everyone's familiar with the "twist tie," that indispensable closure device that secures our garbage bags and clutters the floor of the bread drawer. Bedford Industries, Inc., the largest "twist tie" company in the world, has turned to the craft industry with a new "twist" on ribbon.

First exhibited at the ACCI show in Chicago, Bedford Bendable Ribbon® is available in six widths and six metallic colors. Robert Ludlow, president of the company, believes that designer support of the Bendable Ribbon will gain him market share and is ready and willing to take suggestions for line expansion and novel uses.

Currently Bedford is marketing a line of twenty craft kits and two support leaflets. Kits include wreath making, jewelry making, ornament creation, gift-package additions, and more. All kits have complete instructions and step-by-step illustrations.

—Craft and Needlework, September 1990

The Daily Globe ran this photo with its article: "Bedford Industries president Bob Ludlow displays a Christmas decoration made from Bedford's newest product, wired ribbon. More than 20 kits and ribbon assortments are on sale at Lee's Frame and Craft Shoppe in Worthington."

Bedford Markets Ribbon!

The wired ribbon is actually a larger, prettier variation on the twist ties manufactured by Bedford Industries . . .

"It's unique," Bedford president Bob Ludlow said. "No one else is doing it."

Don't think of bows when you think of this bendable ribbon. Think of spirals ascending into the air; think of banners that no longer hang limply; think of glossy barrettes. Christmas tree ornaments, miniature Christmas trees themselves made of curled ribbons no wider than bread-wrapper twist ties . . .

Three marketing areas include floral shows, craft shows, and visual display companies.

"We have to educate the florists," Ludlow said. "At craft shows we can expose it to large mass merchandisers and also the independent craft stores, which are the backbone of the industry . . ."

Early response has been favorable in all three areas. Ludlow expects all three to continue to expand, although one of the three will probably outdistance the others . . .

—*Worthington Daily Globe*, September 26, 1990

Bedford attended the 1991 HIA (Hobby Industries of America) Show in San Francisco to display Bedford Bendable Ribbon® products. Each year HIA invited exhibitors to submit a product for the "Innovations" display, shown off at the main entrance. Trade and press personnel cast their votes for the most innovative products of the year. Bedford Industries was one of 12 companies to take the "Best of 91." Fairly consistently, Bedford Bendable Ribbon® was picked best product at craft shows and industry contests. "There was a lot of hype," Bob Boushek said, "but never the drive from sales."

Upon commencement of the Gulf War in 1991, Bedford received many requests for yellow tie ribbon. Along with yellow, the company produced a red-white-and-blue tie for patriotic, craft, and decorative themes. The employees mailed President George Bush and Mrs. Barbara Bush a yellow ribbon and a red-white-and-blue ribbon. They included a letter asking the Bush family to display the bows proudly. Making the yellow ribbon was

A red-white-and-blue USA sign lined with yellow ribbons hung on the Bedford building, visible to Interstate 90.

Bedford's way of supporting the troops in the Persian Gulf.

Bedford wanted to do more than buy stock paper from other companies and insert wire into it. It wanted to expand its horizons, to offer custom design and printing applications, and to research printing equipment that might be adaptable to Bedford's needs. The team found a flexographic printing press at the Mark Andy Corporation that could print on films, foils, tissues, papers, and tagboard. The only press available for printing on these substrates was priced just under $1 million. The team purchased a five-color Mark Andy 4200 in May 1991, bringing new possibilities for Bedford Bendable Ribbon®.

To spark interest from craft consumers, Bedford advertised minicraft projects that consumers could purchase through the mail for a dollar. The Bedford team was amazed when it received 30,000 consumer responses to this incentive. The promotion made Bedford Bendable Ribbon® a household name for crafters and hobbyists.

Until 1991, graphics work and plate design for the printing press was done by hand—with a pencil on a drafting table. Now the custom design and printing market grew so rapidly that the engineers and drafters could not keep up while balancing it with their engineering projects. At the same time, Bedford Industries was spending between $75,000 and $100,000 per year on advertising—it wanted more control of its ads and less expense. To resolve these problems, Bedford Industries birthed Bedford Graphics in 1992.

Bedford Graphics was a unique department from its start—everything had previously been done by hand or produced by an outside company. In ten years, it grew from one to three employees on the cutting edge of graphic-design technology. Now known as Bedford Creative, this team does all of Bedford's ads, website graphics, product mock-ups, and company catalogs. Some advertisements have won prestigious Addy Awards—usually granted to the projects of advertising-specific firms. Bedford Creative manages in-house Bedford's 6,000 sets of printing plates for the pressroom, a full video-production system, and most of its digital photography. Contracting with an outside company to do the work done by Bedford Graphics would cost an estimated $400,000 a year. Greater cost control and product versatility for custom graphics has been an important advantage for the company.

In August 1992, Bedford Bendable Ribbon® floral products were displayed at the Silk '92 show in Las Vegas. Competing with thousands of products, Bedford earned a spot as one of the "Ten Trendiest Products" for its "Ivy Entwinement" printed ribbon, a major accomplishment for Bedford and its floral product line. The product was unique in that Bedford simply scanned a piece of ivy and printed it on the ribbon—no other company had thought of it. The project took a few weeks to get going, as the team learned to print photos on the Mark Andy press.

The year 1992 was an anomaly for Bedford—bringing a slow-down of sales. Though the change could be attributed to a recessionary period, Bedford was not used to being in that situation. It did not lose customers or sales to competition; its customers simply needed fewer twist ties. And the craft market did not come together as the team had planned. "We have not been able to figure out how to market craft ribbon profitably," Ludlow explained. "People want it, and it is a good market, but it costs so much to do the marketing. We haven't been able to figure out how to make it pay."

When Bedford first considered the floral market in 1990, little double-wired ribbon was available. Wholesale florists wanted to carry large amounts of decorative wired ribbon, and Bedford was ready. But other companies followed with similar products, and Bedford could not establish a strong position. "It is a good business," Ludlow said, "but it is going to take a lot of innovation on our part to attain anything but slow growth."

The craft market was not as profitable as anticipated. Sales were small and advertising was expensive. "It took $2.00 worth

This craft catalog shows part of almost 50 craft projects sold by Bedford. Each required its own marketing and advertising.

of advertising to get $1.00 in sales," Boushek explained. Production could not keep up with the constantly changing marketplace either. By the time Bedford was able to manufacture a specific ribbon or mass produce a specific craft kit, craft designers wanted something else.

From 1990 to 1994, the commercial marketplace changed dramatically. Large retail chains like Office Depot, Sports Authority, and Circuit City took over. Michaels expanded in the craft industry, closing many of the small "Ma and Pa" shops. Mass retailers went to Asia to find inexpensive craft products.

The floral market began a similar paradigm shift. When Bedford entered the floral market, "Ma and Pa" shops were making 70 to 80 percent of retail floral sales in the United States. Then grocery stores added large floral departments, growing to 30 to 40 percent of retail floral sales and driving many "Ma and Pa" shops out of business. Though mass merchandisers responded well to Bedford's floral ribbon, they were not as interested in American products. Large grocery chains went to China to purchase products instead. The WF & FSA show in Atlanta downsized substantially as most of the buying turned to overseas.

In the wake of industry change, a lot of Bedford Bendable Ribbon® remained in inventory. The Bedford Factory Outlet Store opened in downtown Worthington to sell excess inventory. It was a positive opportunity for the company, providing a clear and rapid understanding of what customers liked and did not like about Bedford ribbon. The store, open four years, served more than 20,000 customers. The average sale was around six dollars; eventually the inventory was depleted, and the store closed.

Ideas from the craft and floral market provided the ladder for a new division—custom products. Floral as a distinct division dissolved, with emphasis moving to banners and ribbons for the visual display market. These used the same technology as floral products but provided new opportunities and new customers demanding custom products, such as Chanel and Lancome™ cosmetics—both sold in the high-end department stores. Neiman Marcus, J. C. Penny's, and Dayton's requested custom ribbons and banners.

The Walt Disney Corporation spotted Bedford's ribbon at an FTD show. It ordered ribbon from other manufacturers but wanted custom printing and labeling. In October, a Bedford presentation showed Disney its standard wired ribbon, along with examples of custom projects. The Bedford team printed Mickey Mouse paper and strung it with wire to take along. In the meeting, the team designed some products on a laptop computer in front of Disney staff members (unusual at that time). Impressed by Bedford's state-of-the-art capabilities and the potential for custom ribbon, the Disney crew decided to sell it with gift wrap in amusement-park shops.

Selling to Disney required a substantial amount of phone contact and follow-up. Getting through the Disney system and working with its character-licensing people took more than a year. The Magic Kingdom®, Epcot®, and MGM Studios, for instance, had individual staffs for parades, outdoor decorating, shop windows, and main-street decorations. This was a complex account.

The effort resulted in a Bedford account with the Disney staff that decorated 320 shop windows. That led to more contacts and further accounts with parade and special events staffs. Bedford produced stickers for events including the Mickey Mouse, Hercules, and Toy Story parades. Ribbon was produced for Main Street USA, Disney stores in malls across the United States, the Grand Floridian Resort, and its giant Christmas tree. Disney went beyond ribbon and twist tie, even purchasing Bedford Plastic Timbers® for walkways. Between 1994 and 1997, Bedford quoted 13 projects for the Disney Corporation.

Though the venture into floral, craft, and custom was not the success Bedford had hoped for, Ludlow and Boushek felt it was a major stepping-stone that brought the company important technological gain. The addition of the Mark Andy printer, for example, would not have been made without the venture into floral, and years later it became one of Bedford's most profitable assets. "Our venture into craft and floral," Boushek revealed, "took what we did with our equipment into a lot of different aspects. What we learned about adhesive led us into skip adhesive and all the other things that we are doing today."

10

Experiment

Y̶ou just peel and stick," a customer stated, trying Bedford's
latest product, "Skip Adhesive." That customer gave the
product the catchy name the Bedford marketing department was
looking for–Peel & Stick® gave rise to another new direction for
Bedford Industries.

Lloyd Tinklenberg was often the bridge between the customer and expanding technology. His engineering background,
coupled with experience in sales, made him an important factor
in many of Bedford's innovations. And with the company's exit of
the craft and floral markets, Bedford once again was looking for
the next big product.

The Bedford sales team took an interest in the coffee industry, which was looking for reclosablility. The market was growing
as specialty coffee grew in popularity and companies like
Starbuck's sprang up across the United States. Bedford worked
hard to get Fresco Coffee, its first coffee customer.

Small coffee roasters began calling Bedford about using
its .315 double-wire tie on coffee bags. The roasters wanted

reclosability and liked the product's features, but lacked a way to put it on a bag. Bedford had a similar product, called the pressure-sensitive adhesive tie, which was used in the medical field. The backside of the pressure-sensitive adhesive tie was coated in glue, allowing it to stick to the bags. But the glue was too expensive for consumer applications.

The Bedford team experimented with different glues. It had learned a lot about glue from the ribbon and floral project and used that as a starting block. As with many of Bedford's earlier projects, the unsuccessful craft and floral endeavor made it possible to develop one of Bedford's more successful products—the Peel & Stick® tie.

The Peel & Stick® concept for bag reclosability.

Peel & Stick® ties used Bedford's traditional .315 tie with adhesive on the backside. As the original name, Skip Adhesive, suggests, the adhesive was applied in an intermittent fashion, leaving nonadhesive areas to cut and fold over on the ends. A release liner was applied over the adhesive. When the release liner was peeled off, by hand or machine, the tie stuck to the bag. The adhesive was set to the size of the bag, with only the nonadhesive ends extending past the edge.

Reflecting years later, Ludlow said the seemingly easy Peel & Stick® production process was not that way at first. The production team struggled with stopping and starting the glue—its first attempts resulted in solid glue on the entire tie. When folded over, the ends stuck to the bag—not the result Bedford wanted. A more promising attempt involved attaching paper to the ends of the tie to cover the excess glue. But this product did not appeal to customers and consumers. In 1991, the engineering and production teams finally found a process to skip the glue to the right spot—the Peel & Stick® tie was born.

With sales just beginning, customers called in to find easier ways to apply the new ties. Some coffee companies applied the closure in quantities of hundreds of thousands, making hand application too labor-intensive. The companies wanted machines that could apply the tie.

Bedford Industries shied away from manufacturing tie-application machinery. Burford Corporation was the major manufacturing company for bakery machinery. A longtime driving force behind the twist-tie market, it had a strong hold and Bedford did not want to make an enemy. Doboy and Plas-Ties also manufactured machinery. They produced small, tabletop-style machines for applying ties to candy bags. Among these companies, the machinery market was satisfied. "It was a smart thing for us to do—staying out of the machine market for a long, long time," Tinklenberg said.

But current twist-tie applicator manufacturers refused to make a machine for coffee roasters, claiming the market was too small. In this, Bedford saw a prime opportunity. The challenge required inventing and perfecting machinery along with creating more demand for the company's products. The engineering staff developed and tested a machine that coffee roasters overwhelmingly accepted. Not only could Bedford profit from the sale of these machines, but the machine's existence also resulted in ad-

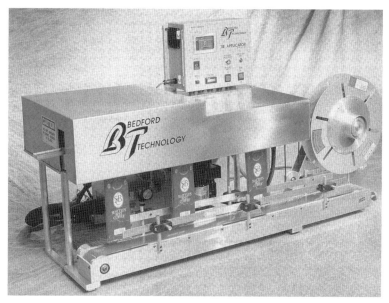

Bedford Technology introduced its first machine—the 2000 Series—in 1992. The name was registered as a trademark in 1995.

ditional tie sales. This led a new division—Bedford Technology.

The first machine, called the 2000 Series, went to Victor Allen Coffee in Madison, Wisconsin. Lloyd Tinklenberg's theory was, "If I have a customer who needs something, then I have something I can work with—use them as a guinea pig. Most customers are happy to do it because they know they are on the cutting edge." In November 1992, *Packaging Digest* ran this story, in part:

Allen's Ties One On

Spills at the supermarket's checkout counter are an irritant to everyone involved—especially when the lost product is a premium quality coffee. To forestall such accidents, Victor Allen's Coffee & Tea, Madison, Wis., has become one of the nation's first coffee roasters to semiautomatically apply tin-tie-type metal ties to flat bags used by consumers buying any of Allen's nearly 40 coffees from bulk.

Alongside its in-store display of 12 bulk bins plus a grinder and supply of l-lb bags, Allen's had provided the same 5½ in, .315 double-wire ties from Bedford Industries, for consumers to use themselves . . .

"For those consumers who removed the strip and placed the tie on the bag properly after grinding or filling beans, the tin-tie was fine," says Allen's plant engineer Marek Kokoszka to PD. "But for others less adept, it was a problem," he adds. "And of course, the ties might be knocked to the floor by a shopper who was in a rush."

That in-store wastage has now been eliminated, along with the cost of the adhesive strip. For the packs made in-plant, even semi-automated application saves labor compared with doing it by hand. Altogether, Kokoszka estimates Allen's is saving about 33 cents/bag . . .

"Customers were happy because at least they had something—the only alternative was doing it by hand," Tinklenberg said. At the retail bakers' show in California, response to the new .315 tie machine was more positive than expected. In fact, Bedford sold three machines to Starbuck's Coffee right away.

At trade shows, big-name brands and bakeries approached Bedford, wanting a more automated machine. Bedford was asked to start developing a complete system that would integrate the machine into the process of filling the bag—apply a tie, fold the bag, and bend the tie ends—more than Bedford had anticipated upon entering the coffee-machinery market. *Minnesota Technology* briefly described Bedford Technology's purpose:

> Designed for use in conjunction with packagers' form-and-fill equipment, Bedford's machines significantly reduce the need for repetitive hand labor. They target, according to Ludlow, a promising niche in the market—smaller gourmet coffee makers, for example, who don't need or can't afford the large, multipurpose packaging machines made in Europe, but could make good use of a labor-saving device that costs a fraction of

the big machines. "We're really just starting out this year," says Ludlow. "Next year we hope the machinery will account for about 10 percent of our business."

In 1993, Bedford met the demand of larger bakeries with the Series 4000H, a fully automated tie applicator. Using the trade-marked slogan, "Innovation in Motion®," Bedford developed an array of machines for varied packaging applications. The team performed a number of experiments, searching for new machinery to fill gaps in the marketplace. At one point, the engineers had a two-story, form-fill sealing machine inside the Bedford factory—just to figure out how it worked. Another contribution to the machinery lineup was the stand-up Ring Tier in 1996. The Ring Tier had been developed for bundling objects, such as coils of hoses and certain vegetables, with twist tie.

One morning, Ludlow went into the Bedford graphics department. He told artists John Linquist and Deb Houseman that he wanted a character for Bedford—like that of California Raisins™. A week later, in the middle of night, Linquist had a dream about a bag with a cape, resembling Superman. When he woke

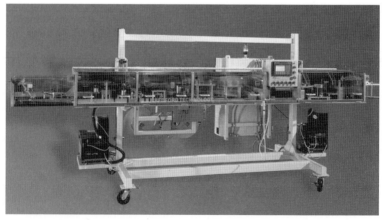

The 4100 Series machine, above, succeeded the 4000H in 1993.

Minnesota Technology ran a story about Bedford diversification, with this shot of Bob Ludlow and a new machine, 1993. (Dan Vogel photo)

from the dream, he drew "Bag Man." The following day, Linquist brought his drawing into Bedford and told the story to Houseman. As they were laughing about the dream, Ludlow walked in. He liked what he heard.

Linquist drew different versions of "Bagman Bob." The idea did not stop there but continued to evolve. Ludlow wanted an illustration of Bagman Bob coming down a conveyor belt with a frown, going through a Bedford Technology® machine, and coming out the other side with a twist tie and a smile on his face.

Bedford was buying a new trade show booth at the same time. The company that made the booths also sold animatronics—animated displays for theme parks and museums. Bedford hired the company to build an animated Bagman Bob—one that could sing and talk. To make sure customers understood that Bedford sold the tie but not the bags, another company was hired to make a parody of the song "Unforgettable." Its new words: "I'm

Bedford created a reclosability spokesman—Bagman Bob.

Reclosable." Bagman Bob made his first and only appearance at the PMMI show in Chicago because the continual play of the song got on everyone's nerves.

The machinery market opened up further for Bedford when American Design and Packaging approached it with an offer to sell in 1997. Previously known as Doboy Machinery Company, it was one of the original twist-tie machinery manufacturers focusing on smaller equipment. Bedford Industries was interested in incorporating the Doboy products into its growing line of machinery and purchased the Doboy assets, including its super-tying stand-up and mini-tying tabletop units.

Bedford Technology grew so large that, by 1998, it was no longer a sideline but a main focus of the company. Much of Bedford's time was spent building machines for orders, rarely giving the engineering staff time to take care of twist-tie and production projects.

Ludlow entertained the idea of spinning the division into its own company because Bedford Industries was too busy to focus on both simultaneously. In the marketing department, there were two different philosophies—one for selling ties and another for selling machinery. "You can't wear two hats at the same time," Boushek said. Also, machine-manufacturing companies that wanted to build machines to apply twist tie refused to work with Bedford Industries in the development process as long as it too made large, automated machinery.

On October 1, 1998, Bedford Industries, Inc., announced the sale of Bedford Technology and the recycled plastic lumber division to four of its engineers. The operation was moved to a new location on the east side of Worthington. Sixteen employees transferred with the sale, including half of the Bedford Industries engineering staff.

"This sale was made because we felt it would be better for the large machinery division to be separate from Bedford Industries, Inc.," Ludlow said. "When designing a new machine in an engineering system for a large food manufacturer, you have to spend all of your time concentrating on the project. At Bedford Industries, the engineers were under the additional pressure of solving everyday tie-production problems as well. If the business was separate, there could be full concentration on the design of machines and systems."

"Plastic lumber was thrown in as a carrot," Bob Boushek explained. It had consistent and rapidly growing sales and provided an instant source of income to Bedford Technology, LLC. The lumber division also did not get adequate attention at Bedford Industries.

Bedford Technology started with 20 employees. It boasted an experienced staff of engineers, designers, sales personnel, and machinists. It quickly built a fully equipped machine shop, making its own machinery parts. The new company kept its shop busy with custom jobs from customers in the surrounding area. Bedford Plastic Timbers® continued to grow, adding state-of-the-art production lines and developing a subsidiary called ForeSite Designs™ for the manufacture of outdoor furniture.

Bedford Industries experienced no decrease in sales or growth as a result of the sale, which helped the company refocus on its core products and move deeper into new markets. The company held onto the small machinery it had purchased from American Design and Packaging. It complemented Bedford Industries products, without overwhelming them. Once again, Bedford returned to the twist tie.

11

Design and upgrade

On April 22, 1994, Bedford received a call from Constable Dave Black, a forensics specialist with the Delta police force in British Columbia, Canada. He was investigating a homicide and had a few questions for Bedford.

He explained that a woman had been murdered, her body put inside two trash bags, finally surrounded with a third, orange, trash bag–the interior bag tied with a twist tie. Constable Black traced the orange trash bags to First Brands Corporation, finding Bedford to be the manufacturer of the twist ties. These specific bags were grouped in a five-pack with red double-wire gang ties, printed with the GLAD® logo on the reverse side.

The Delta police had a suspect and found a box of trash bags and ties at the suspect's home. They wanted to find a match between these materials and the ones found at the crime scene. Constable Black wanted to know how the ties were produced and about their characteristics. Producing the proper identification, Constable Black asked to come to Minnesota and see how the twist ties were manufactured.

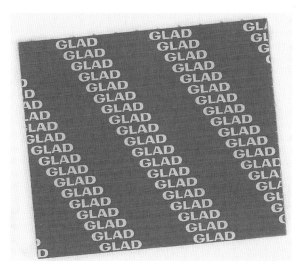

*The GLAD® logos on the gang ties were evenly spaced,
but the perforations were not.*

On June 23, Constable Black arrived at Bedford Industries with microscope in hand. He had studied the tie and concluded there was a strong possibility the tie found at the crime scene could be matched with those at the suspect's home. The key was the unpredictability of Bedford ties. The slit and serration process, allowing the ties to tear away, produced a random pattern. The GLAD® logos on the reverse side were printed diagonally, in a continual pattern, evenly spaced to fill the entire side. Constable Black hoped this might serve as a "fingerprint" match to the ties still in the box. Looking at the twist tie under a microscope, he found lines, or impressions, in the plastic that were perpendicular to the wire. If the lines in the plastic matched the printing and slit/serration, the police could be in luck.

A year later, on August 17, 1995, Bob Ludlow received a letter from Constable Black. He wrote telling Bedford the Delta police had finalized successful prosecution of the case. Thanks to the twist tie, the world is a safer place!

In the 1980s and 1990s, many manufacturers, including those in the twist-tie industry, faced great change. Companies like Mobil and First Brands worked to eliminate the twist tie. Many of the original twist-tie companies in the country closed their doors—going out of business or absorbed by larger firms.

"We in the manufacturing industry really don't know if we are doing everything right in our day-to-day decisions. I believe the only true test as to who makes the better decision is who survives and who does not survive. The companies that have survived have satisfied their customers and markets and must have been doing a better job than the companies who declined or disappeared. A person never knows whether his company is going in the right direction strategically until he compares it with competitors. I think Bedford is doing the better job since it has survived and grown, where the rest of the industry has shrunk or been sold because sales were slipping. If such a method of keeping score is valid, I think everyone at Bedford should be congratulated. It is a combination of everything—quality, reasonable pricing, continuous improvements, on-time deliveries, courteous phone relationships, new products, etc.—that keeps customers coming back," Bob Ludlow said.

Bedford acquired Plas-Ties in 1974 and American Design and Manufacturing in 1997. It made no other major acquisitions in that period, but as other manufacturers dropped out in the late 1990s, Bedford purchased their twist-tie assets. Each of these approached Bedford Industries, offering to sell. Bedford never made the first move. This gave Bedford Industries the opportunity to learn from the mistakes of other companies and to see what it did correctly as well.

One of these, St. Regis Paper, was the large company, originally a major producer of bread bags, from which Bedford purchased the Polytray thermo-forming line in 1979. When the twist-tie industry began to grow in the late 1960s, St. Regis Paper developed a bread-bag twist-tie line to complement its bag-manufacturing capabilities. Though it had a full twist-tie line at one time, St. Regis scaled down after a few years because its twist-tie division was an inconvenience for the large company. To simplify its process, St. Regis offered only a 10-inch spool of twist tie. Even when customers wanted something different, St. Regis did not provide options. Instead, the large company referred these customers to Bedford, which was small enough to concentrate on specialized, short-run products.

St. Regis left the twist-tie industry because the 10-inch spool market was not enough to sustain its twist-tie division. In the early 1980s, it combined with Tite Ties (later sold to Middletown Packaging), one of the early twist-tie companies, to form a single company under Bettendorf Stanford, which was already involved in the bakery industry—manufacturing blades used to slice bread. Bettendorf Stanford entered the twist-tie business with a lot of connections, making it a major competitor in the bakery industry.

St. Regis and Middletown sold about $4 million each in twist tie, but the combined company struggled after the merger. Bettendorf Stanford as a whole was sold and resold again, causing the company to drop from about $8 million to just $500,000 in sales. Its equipment was outdated. With capacity only for bread-bag ties, it could not produce gang ties and double-wire ties, or provide specialty applications. Versatile companies like Bedford Industries gained more of the twist-tie market, leaving Bettendorf Stanford stuck with uncompetitive equipment.

In 1994, Bettendorf Stanford approached Bedford Industries with an offer to sell. Accepting the offer, Bedford purchased

*Ludlow stood in the entrance to Bettendorf Stanford, 1994. A hole in
the side of the building provided the only passageway for equipment.*

Bettendorf Stanford's twist-tie manufacturing equipment and
customer lists. But Bedford employees chose not to use the out-
of-date equipment acquired in the purchase.

In November 1999, Bedford learned that a twist-tie manufacturing company in Vancouver, British Columbia, Canada, was
dissolving its operation. David Heise Sales, Ltd., was a low-
profile name in the twist-tie industry but a company that had
been in business for many years. It was known for making small
spools and identification ties, but it had begun manufacturing
single-cut ties and gang ties.

Bob Boushek and Dave Reker had visited the facility in an-
ticipation of acquiring the business. It was a small plant with
slow, old equipment. Boushek assumed that little money had
been invested in improving the product lines. To remove the machinery from the industry and acquire David Heise Sales' customer list, Bedford submitted a bid for the assets and won.

Boushek said, "This is a good example of why a company needs to keep investing in its future. Continuous upgrading of our equipment and always looking for new markets has helped make Bedford what it is today. [Employee] cooperation in always striving to do better, making quality products, and willingness to work on new products are what makes it happen. Our future . . . is geared towards making new and exciting things happen."

Tom Haddock believed that putting money into equipment to improve the process was one of the keys to Bedford's success and longevity. Bedford invested the money because it had pride in its product, pride in the twist tie.

"You'd wonder sometimes whether Bob Ludlow was being practical, but I trusted him," Haddock explained. In hindsight, the continued upgrade of Bedford equipment was one of its greatest assets—arguably what allowed Bedford to thrive when many twist-tie companies failed. Technological advantage gave the company the capability to adapt to new products and fill small niches.

One niche that Bedford Industries could not have entered without a strong technological advantage is the field of medical products. For years, Bedford sold tie to 3M Company and other companies to use on face masks. Requests came in regarding further medical ideas, giving the Bedford team a broader market for its product. Bedford met the challenge by developing specialty ties for medical face masks and surgical drapes with exclusive adhesives blended specifically for medical applications. The medical-tie market took off rapidly, prodding Bedford to introduce a full product line—Bedford Bendable Components®.

In 2001, Phil Merlin, president of Alcar Industries, one of Bedford's longtime competitors and rivals, called Bob Ludlow. He wanted to sell his company and offered it to Bedford. Acquiring Alcar, one of Bedford's most challenging competitors, was an opportunity Bedford Industries could not refuse. Merlin and Ludlow had spoken of a purchase in years past, but Merlin set his price higher than Bedford was willing to take. Now Merlin was ready to sell at a reasonable price.

After the sale, Bedford employees rented a Greyhound bus to travel to Newburgh, New York, and clean out the Alcar facility. Some manufacturing equipment was salvageable, but most of the technology, less advanced than Bedford's, had limited Alcar's capabilities.

The Alcar Industries acquisition was significant for several reasons. First, it brought a considerable number of East Coast sales to Bedford. Second, and more important, it symbolized Bedford's leadership in the twist-tie industry and enforced Bedford Industries as the world's leading twist-tie producer. It was a profitable acquisition that paid for itself within three years.

Dale Holmes, Keith Fisher, and Matt Van Muyden looked on and learned as Alcar employees demonstrated their production process, 2001.

Kim Milbrandt had left Bedford with the sale of the container division to Amoco in 1988. In 1998, he rejoined Bedford as president, and he was among the employees traveling to Alcar. He remembered the staff at Alcar commenting on the attitude and work ethic of Bedford employees: "They could not believe how focused and hard-working everyone was—constant supervision was not needed. They were amazed at how everyone got along so well and acted like one big, happy family. One person said this was a real eye-opener for what other companies might be like."

Milbrandt heard the greatest compliment during final negotiations at the attorney's office: "At one point, there was a concern among the Alcar owners about possible errors in inventory evaluation. The attorney suggested that another legal document be constructed to protect Alcar in case any errors or omissions occurred. Bob Ludlow intervened and said that Bedford would financially correct any errors. The attorney insisted that a document be created, but Phil Merlin, Alcar's president, said, 'If Bob Ludlow gives his word, that is good enough for me!'" The

Longtime industry rivals Phil Merlin, president of Alcar Industries, and Bob Ludlow, upon Bedford's acquisition of Alcar, 2001.

compliment, Milbrandt suggested, reflected the high level of integrity upon which Bedford was founded.

*Keith Fisher and Mike Steffl dismantled a machine
acquired in Canada in 2003.*

With the economy in a slow period, Bedford continued to grow despite the economic odds against it. Not only did it gain more customers and develop a number of new products, but it also made two more acquisitions in the following six months— Twist Tie Manufacturing, Inc., and Leonard James Devices, Ltd., the last two twist-tie manufacturers in Canada. The firms were small and held only old equipment. The age of small twist-tie manufacturers was coming to a close.

12

Breakthrough

S he said that if I could find her a purple engagement ring, she
would marry me." This was one of the more unusual requests received by the sales department for a twist tie. A man
wanted a purple twist tie to win the heart of his beloved. The in-
house sales department designed one and shipped it off in a small
jewelry box. They never heard the result, but they never received
a complaint, either.

Bedford believed it could better satisfy customers' needs in
supermarkets. Enter Twist Ease Corporation, of Minneapolis, in
1992, which wished to develop a twist-tie dispenser for use in
produce departments. Many supermarkets were switching from
bulk twist-ties (cut ties in cups) to Kwik Lok Corporation's tabs
on wire rods. Prompting the switch were consumer spills of twist
ties into the produce; supermarkets spent a lot of time cleaning
them up. Together, Bedford and Twist Ease developed a product
that eliminated Kwik Lok tabs from the produce section.

Bedford had always been in supermarkets—most commonly
the bakeries. In the garbage-bag industry, some companies

began integrating cinching devices into bags, but twist ties were still common. Bedford twist ties became popular in the produce department, due to the Twist Ease dispenser. Then tags and labels began to appear on fruits and vegetables—a stage Bedford thought it could compete on. Bedford had a printing press and the knowledge to create a quality product.

The time was perfect because the produce industry and supermarkets were experiencing problems in 1995. With the wide offering of fruits and vegetables on the market, few cashiers and customers knew the name of every vegetable. Sometimes a checkout employee spent several minutes looking up a product name to match it with the proper price—a problem supermarkets wanted to change. Supermarkets required that all produce have an attached bar code (UPC number) for scanning at the register and a four-digit PLU (product look-up) number in case the bar code did not scan. Some of the more progressive supermarkets

Snap-A-Tag® and Bib Ties® on produce, 1995.

refused delivery of produce if it was not marked. By the time the grower received it back, the produce was worthless.

This revolutionized the way the produce industry operated and led to a rush to standardize codes and numbers for produce across the country. Bok choy, napa cabbage, and asparagus each were given a separate but universal PLU number and UPC code. Produce growers tried to comply with these standards and provide a tag acceptable to consumers—all within two months.

In a unique position to offer produce ties and tags quickly because of its in-house art department, Bedford scrambled to make samples. It seemed an easy product to integrate into the Bedford mix, but that was not the case. Each grower and each commodity needed a different produce tie. Some growers and supermarkets wanted personalized ties and tags, while some wanted generic ones. Certain regions needed dual languages for selling internationally or in particular ethnic regions.

"Regardless of how confusing things were in the marketplace, there was a big market developing rapidly in our country and in Canada," Ludlow explained. "It was all being forced down the throats of growers by the supermarkets, so it was going to take place whether the growers wanted to do it or not. The faster Bedford could react, the bigger the share of the market we could gain. The bigger market share we got, the better the price in the future and the more difficult it would be for anyone to move us out of the market."

Supermarkets conducted studies showing that 20 to 30 percent more produce was sold if there was a label or recipe attached to it. Bedford knew it had a market that was not merely a fad. Market potential led to experimentation and sampling of Bedford's products in 1995. Bedford adapted a half-inch twist tie for produce and created two new product lines called Flag

Ties® and Bib Ties®. Both involved gluing a tag onto twist tie for greater labeling and identification space.

"We plunged into a new product, finding ourselves as sudden leaders in a market we didn't understand," Ludlow said. "Even as new as we were in this area, we were well ahead of the competition for ties and tags utilizing UPC bar codes and PLU numbers. Our quality and durability was the best in the marketplace and the success of our 'Taste of Texas' tags [for instance] exceeded all expectations."

The market moved quickly, often leaving employees with the feeling they did not know where Bedford was heading or what direction the market would take. As Ludlow described it, Bedford and the new market were "the blind leading the blind." Bedford was challenged to enter a market that it did not understand, as it provided the best price on products that were expensive to make.

The all-plastic, wireless twist tie was still not accomplished by 1997, though the team wanted to make it. It had been on the back burner for many years. Tom Haddock headed up the project but left in 1986 to work for Ball Plastics. Bob Ludlow thought the wireless tie was close and that, with Haddock's help, it could be ready to sell in a month or two. Haddock came back to work for Bedford Industries in 1997, but the wireless tie was *not* ready in two months—it took four more years of work. The dream came into fruition in 2001 when the engineering staff invented a variety of wireless tie that would perform in the bakery using Burford Corporation machinery.

Meanwhile, Bedford Industries owned the building that housed Bedford Plastics in Sioux Falls. Amoco rented, not purchased, it from Bedford. Amoco later sold its high-performance packaging division (formerly Bedford Plastics) to Anchor Packaging, Inc., which then dissolved the operation. Bedford was left

Bedford Industries gave itself a facelift with a new logo in 2001.

with the building, which it used as a warehouse, though the distance between facilities was inconvenient. In 2002, Bedford found a buyer interested in purchasing the building—which meant Bedford would have to increase its storage space elsewhere. As the sale went through, the Bedford team was planning the next addition to the main facility in Worthington. By winter 2002, Bedford had completed a new 60,000-square-foot warehouse and shipping center.

In a speech to employees celebrating the opening of the new facility, Ludlow remarked on Bedford's history of building expansions and the meaning behind this latest one. "This building symbolizes not only a needed expansion, but a commitment to Worthington and to the Bedford employees. Bedford could be anywhere, so it is more of a commitment to you employees who live in the Worthington area. This commitment to keep Bedford viable and growing as an organization is a continuing effort to offer you a decent place to work so that you can raise your families and work among friends."

Many of Bedford's accomplishments have become day-to-day operations—precision-wound spoolless tie, Peel & Stick®, even the twist-tie process itself. The company has invented processes meriting more than 38 patents and 35 trademarks. In 30 years of running three shifts per day, it has never backlogged more than 48 hours' worth of twist-tie orders.

The pace of Bedford Industries' progress has not let up. Many employees have commented that Bedford has more happening today than ever before.

So, where is Bedford at the end of 2004? Bedford Bendable Components® has introduced the medical industry to the twist tie. Bedford works with many large medical-supply companies on face masks, colostomy bags, and other products.

The R-Line of small machinery has grown beyond the Mini Bedford Tie-R® and Super Bedford Tie-R®. The tabletop-sized Apply-R machine, designed to apply Peel & Stick® or Fold N Close® ties to coffee bags, has proved popular—Bedford sold 19 machines in the first five months of production. A variety of other tabletop application machines is slated for introduction soon.

Bedford has adapted an identification tag for almost every fruit and vegetable. The original Flag Ties®, Bib Ties®, and Snap-A-Tags® are available in many shapes and sizes. They have given rise to new methods for attaching identification tags to produce. The Cinch Band® was developed for radicchio and larger vegetables.

Bedford developed the ElastiTag™, one of its newest and most exciting products, as the result of a progression of the following products building on each other. The Bib Ties® were at-

The Bedford Industries factory after several expansions, 2004.

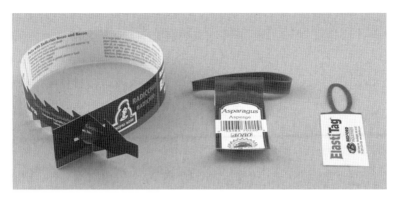

Some of Bedford's latest identification tags:
(left to right) the Cinch Band®, Band Tag, and ElastiTag™, 2004.

tached to fruits and vegetables with a twist tie. Some fruits and vegetables swell after harvest or require a more flexible attachment than a twist tie; that need was fulfilled with the Snap-A-Tag®, a tag that is snapped on to a rubber band. A more convenient tag called the Band Tag was next. The Band Tag integrated the identification tag with the rubber band. Finally (or maybe not!), Bedford developed the ElastiTag™—a one-piece tag and elastic loop.

The ElastiTag™ has exceeded the expectations of customers and is used in a large market beyond the produce industry. Examples of its applications include retail, floral, automotive labeling, and product promotion. Bedford has developed the capability of integrating RFID (radio frequency identification) into the ElastiTag™ for advanced identification needs. The ElastiTag™ is following in the footsteps of Bedford's big breakthroughs.

Three new centers are growing to meet the latest demands for Bedford's products. Bedford Innovative, a research center and testing lab, pushes Bedford's progress on twist-tie and packaging knowledge. Bedford Innovative has made Bedford an adhesive specialist in the process of finding adhesives that will bond tags and ties to the many varieties of papers, plastics, and lamination coatings found on current packaging—even developing its own proprietary adhesives. The research center is constantly improving the twist tie and wireless tie through the use of its experimental single- and twin-screw extruders. Bedford Innovative is becoming recognized for its capabilities, with outside companies often contracting for research and development.

Recycling is one of Bedford's latest endeavors— to create a twist tie from Bedford's waste. Employees are working to develop a process for recycling plastic discarded during the twist-tie production process. The wire is separated from the plastic, and the material is ground into reusable resin.

Finally, Bedford Creative's printing capabilities have grown with the addition of two more Mark Andy flexographic presses. The presses run almost full time to keep up with demand. This center recently purchased a full-color, digital vinyl press, offering quicker service. With the combination of Bedford Creative and printing capabilities, Bedford has a competitive printing house. It has even contracted its designing and printing services to outside businesses.

Bedford is planning the further expansion of the Rowe Avenue facility. Drawings and plans exist for two state-of-the-art production areas, two more warehouses, and a new office complex. When planned expansions are complete, the Bedford campus will extend about a quarter-mile along Interstate 90.

Some of these ideas may fail. Some may be big breakthroughs. Some may fall victim to stronger ideas. That is the beauty of Bedford's history and its future.

Epilogue

W ho would have guessed from the company's origins in 1966 that it would become what it is today? Bedford has grown from a small, green garage to a state-of-the-art, 143,000-square-foot facility. It has improved the twist-tie process and revolutionized microwavable packaging. After struggling to print the date on a twist tie, Bedford now does nine-color, flexographic printing. The company has taken its products from garbage bags and bakeries to gourmet coffee and surgical facilities. Bedford Industries has accomplished a great deal, and its future seems bright.

The answer to the question raised in the prologue—"What makes Bedford different from other manufacturing firms?"—is innovation. Bedford Industries has innovated itself. Small twist-tie companies selling their assets to Bedford affirm the company's progress. But they also leave the daunting feeling that twist-tie companies cannot stay in the market.

"People do not understand the constant change we have had to do to stay alive," Bob Ludlow says. "Over the years we have

purchased the manufacturing assets of five other twist-tie manufacturers who couldn't change fast enough and had to quit."

Bedford has matched its innovation to changing markets.
Walking into a supermarket now, one has trouble finding twist
ties on more than a few trash bags. In other areas, Ziploc® has
taken most of Bedford's bag-closure business. Twist ties used by
major cracker companies—Nabisco, Keebler, and Sunshine® (a
brand of The Kellogg Company)—have disappeared as well.

"Though phasing out some products, we have been able to
be first in line to capture emerging markets," Ludlow explains.
The bakery market has steadily held to the twist tie, and on the
East Coast especially, one has difficulty finding any bakeries using ties that are not Bedford's. Produce aisles in supermarkets
are riddled with Bedford identification ties and tags. Few produce departments are without them. Bedford has also capitalized
on emerging markets including gourmet-coffee bags and medical
face masks. Today, Bedford Industries dominates both of these
markets.

Though innovation is an underlying theme for Bedford Industries, the company has also been dominated by the core values of "the Bedford family."

The story of Bedford Industries is more about people than a
business or a product. The people have defined the direction and
made the innovations. One of Bedford Industries' greatest
achievements is the loyalty of the employees—over half of them
working at Bedford for 10 to 15 years. John Van Ede, who vowed
not to work in manufacturing at all, testifies that he has always
enjoyed working at Bedford. "You'll never find a finer place to
work," he has said. "And that's why people stay."

Bedford Industries has continually reinvented itself and it
products and come out stronger. But the problem that presents

itself here is how to end a story that does not end? One of Bob Ludlow's favorite sayings is, "There are no problems, only opportunities." Maybe this is another opportunity to dream about the future of Bedford Industries.

Ludlow is often asked whether Bedford's future will remain as strong as its past. He replies, "I am confident it will, if we continue to be competitive, innovative, and quick to respond." If it is true that history repeats itself, this book is more than a testament to Bedford's past. It is a promise for the future.

Afterword

by Robert Ludlow

Thinking back on the 38 years of Bedford Industries' existence—on its evolution from employees creating machines
with junkyard parts to a company of about 200 people manufacturing and selling products worldwide—one has to reflect on why
Bedford succeeded while so many other companies have come
and gone during this time.

There was no body of knowledge on how to make a twist tie
in the literature or in the minds of the first few employees or me.
Of course, the extrusion of wire was standard practice in the
wire-coating industry, and putting wings on a plastic-coated wire
took it one step farther. But the exact art or technology of how to
do this was unknown to any of us. This and the evolution of a
thousand variations of the original twist tie could never be predicted. One has to look to the people to find and appreciate the
answer. It is a tribute to the ingenuity of the employees at
Bedford who searched the junkyard across the street for pulleys,
gears, bearings, and so forth to assemble machines that would
make the twist-tie configurations they had in mind.

That kind of ingenuity has continued to this day—even though we now have graduate engineers and gifted designers—problem solving and ideas about how to make things work come from all employees. If a customer has a request for a new variation of our products, we don't necessarily make an engineering project of it. We (including the engineers) often go to several of the line or quality-control employees with a consumer request, for input and ideas as a primary step towards a successful solution. More than 50 percent of Bedford's people have worked for Bedford for more than 10 years, and more than 20 percent have worked for us for 20 years—that is a tremendous body of knowledge.

When a request comes in from a sales-call report or a telephone call, be it a problem or a new idea, we often gather people from the manufacturing floor for ideas or input on how suggestions best fit into our manufacturing capabilities. We wish to give all of the people at Bedford credit for a major part of its successful 38-and-counting years.

For Bedford's success, I especially give credit to Robert Boushek, Bedford's vice president and general manager from 1973 to 2004. He is the one person who had the greatest managerial influence in Bedford's success. Bob and I have said to each other many times over the years: "We dodged that bullet today," or "Divine Providence was looking out for us today." Both of us hold a deep belief that God (Divine Providence to some) has had a guiding and guarding hand in the building of Bedford Industries over these past years—so that the right employees came on board at the right time, the breakthroughs in manufacturing problems were timely, the fortunate phone call came out of the blue, and the customer paid the bill early so we could meet our payroll. Many people would say these things result from hard work and management skill, but I believe, and I'm sure Bob Boushek would agree with me, that too many good things happened and too many tough problems (beyond our expertise) were licked for the credit to be ours.

I never go into the plant on weekends when everything is quiet without thanking God for placing me as a steward of Bedford and thanking Him for giving me an occupation I enjoy. This business has given Pat and me a good life with the benefits of educating our children and enabling us to modestly support organizations and events we believe worthwhile—all beyond my ability or expertise. Of course, people who know me say Pat, who balances my shortcomings, is the one largely responsible for much of Bedford's 38 years.

For all this I thank God.

Appendices

Bedford Timeline

1966   Bedford, founded in fall, produces plastic twist tie

1967   Incorporates and makes first tie sales

1968   Expands to hatchery building

1971   Produces plastic/paper tie and gang ties

1972   Plans new building

1973   Completes construction of Rowe Avenue facility by October

1974   Invents double-wire ties; acquires the twist-tie manufacturing assets of Plas-Ties Corporation

1975   Begins research into thermoforming for making an all-plastic, wireless tie; makes industry breakthrough with invention of spoolless tie

1976   Conducts market research regarding polypropylene lids

1977   Purchases Thermoline® thermoformer for production of lids; team begins intensive study of European thermoforming technology

1978   Expands Rowe Avenue facility for thermoforming and research and development

1979   Purchases St. Regis Paper Company's tray line

1980   Begins drawing wire in old hatchery facility

1981   Bedford Plastics, Inc., takes delivery of Gabler pressure-forming equipment

1982   Begins production of SPPF containers; double-wire market grows

1984   Bedford Plastics moves to Sioux Falls, South Dakota; Bedford Industries produces more than a million miles of tie in one year

1985   Bedford Plastics makes industry breakthrough with CPET containers

1988   Amoco acquires manufacturing assets of Bedford Plastics; Bedford founds Bedford Transportation

1990   Creates Bedford Bendable Ribbon®

1991   Begins recycling work with Bedford Plastic Timbers®; purchases Mark Andy flexographic printing press

1992   Creates Bedford Technology with first sale of a 2000 series machine; establishes Bedford Graphics as in-house design and advertising department

1994   Acquires manufacturing assets of Bettendorf Stanford, Inc.; establishes custom products division

1995   Enters produce market

1997   Acquires manufacturing assets of American Design and Packaging

1998   Group of Bedford engineers purchases Bedford Technology and its trademark, registered in 1995

1999   Acquires manufacturing assets of David Heise Sales, Ltd.

2001   Acquires manufacturing assets of Alcar Industries, Inc.

2002   Sells Sioux Falls warehouse and constructs new warehouse in Worthington

2003   Acquires manufacturing assets of two Canadian twist-tie companies—Twist Tie Manufacturing and Leonard James Devices

Tie Facts and Figures

Year	Twist ties per day (millions of feet)	Times around earth per year (24,900 miles)	Round trips to moon per year (477,680 miles)
1974	N/A	14.0	0.73
1975	N/A	15.0	0.78
1976	N/A	20.5	1.07
1977	13.3	26.0	1.36
1978	15.8	30.9	1.61
1979	18.1	36.6	1.91
1980	18.5	35.1	1.83
1981	19.7	37.8	1.97
1982	19.4	36.7	1.91
1983	19.3	37.1	1.93
1984	20.4	38.9	2.03
1985	21.8	42.5	2.21
1986	21.6	42.3	2.21
1987	21.2	40.6	2.11
1988	23.5	46.5	2.42
1989	21.6	41.6	2.17
1990	19.9	38.2	1.99
1990	20.0	38.4	2.00
1991	19.0	36.4	1.90
1992	20.1	39.0	2.03
1993	22.7	44.1	2.30
1994	22.6	44.4	2.31
1995	21.8	42.0	2.19
1996	23.7	45.7	2.38
1997	22.8	43.9	2.29
1998	24.6	47.4	2.47
1999	28.2	54.7	2.85
2000	29.7	57.6	3.00
2001	25.4	48.7	2.54
2002	27.5	52.7	2.75
2003	28.0	53.9	2.81

Author's Note: While researching the Bedford Industries story, I began to wonder about the origins of the twist tie. When I found no written history, I decided, as a side project, to write a brief but definitive history of the twist tie's start.

The credit for this history goes to key figures in the twist-tie industry who graciously provided recollections and bridged the gaps in information:

- Luis Contreras—Plas-Ties Corporation, president (1985–present)
- Seymour Glustein—Twist Tie Manufacturing, Inc., president (1964–2001)
- Don Ivey—Burford Corporation, sales manager (1965–present)
- Robert Lauro—Bedford Industries, regional sales manager (1983–present)
- Robert Ludlow—Bedford Industries, Inc., president (1966–2000) and CEO (1966–present)
- Philip Merlin—Alcar Industries, president (1966–2001)
- William D. Patrick—Package Containers, Inc., past sales manager and current chairman of the board
- Eugene Story—Plas-Ties Corporation, sales manager (1988–1997); Bedford Industries, regional sales manager (1997–present)
- Robert R. Whiting—Plas-Ties Corporation, president (1974–1979)

I hope this brief history is a catalyst for gathering more information, and I welcome corrections and additions.

A Twist of History

The twist tie is a remarkable piece of packaging, though most consumers take little notice of it. It has allowed for conveniences that are often taken for granted, such as keeping bread fresh, sealing a bag of trash, or identifying an item of produce in the grocery aisle.

One can find twist ties anywhere. Go into any supermarket and you will see the twist tie on a variety of products—candies, frozen food, and gourmet coffee, just to name a few. This phenomenon is not limited to the United States but is present around the world. The twist tie lives in almost every country.

That begs the question "How many twist ties exist in the world?" In a single year, Bedford Industries, the world's leading manufacturer of twist ties, alone produces enough twist-tie ribbon to make three round trips to the moon! So each year, millions of miles of twist tie enter the world.

The story of the twist tie is as unique as the product itself—one evolving in three separate industries: agriculture, bakery, and trash bags. The story is compelling because the twist tie is such a small, often unthought-of item, but it has achieved universal appeal in just 60 years..

Agriculture

While the exact date is unknown, the twist tie was born in California in the late 1930s. Raffia, a grass then used to bundle produce, seemed indispensable to produce growers. But the South American import was becoming increasingly scarce, and growers on the West Coast were in need of a substitute.

Germain's Seed and Plant[1] (changed to Germain's, Inc., in 1947) was a manufacturer and distributor of produce products. Ross Gast, one of Germain's employees, found a solution to the raffia dilemma. He thought growers could use a wire covered in paper instead. His product, originally "Twist-Ems," was used to bundle produce and tie plants to stakes.

Twist-Ems were a successful substitute for raffia. Demand for Twist-Ems grew rapidly as raffia became unavailable at the beginning of World War II.

Walter R. Schindler[2] is credited with two patents for the production of "Twist-Ems." His first twist-tie machine (U.S. Patent #2,290,386) ran 25 wires through a tank of asphalt. The asphalt-covered wires were rolled between two pieces of paper. The wired paper was slit into individual wires, and a roller with knives on it cut the ties to a certain length.

Schindler's second machine (U.S. Patent #2,371,357) was an improvement over the first. Instead of rolling the wire between two pieces of paper, the new Schindler machine folded one piece of paper to sandwich the wire.

In the late 1940s, Paul Halstead, of Los Angeles, saw Germain's twist-tie machine and thought he could improve it. Halstead believed he could build a machine (U.S. Patent #2,732,001) to make one twist tie at a time—of higher quality and at a faster rate of production. He used one piece of paper—glued and folded. But during the development stage, he began to run out of money.

---

1. Germain's was founded in 1871 as Germain's Fruit. The name was changed to Germain's Seed and Plant in 1909.
2. Walter R. Schindler probably was a Germain's employee or otherwise connected to the company, but this could not be verified.

Halstead knew some people at Package Containers, Inc., in Canby, Oregon. The company manufactured paper bags for the produce and retail industries. The paper twist tie was a natural product for this paper-bag company to acquire. Package Containers bought Halstead's machine and brought him to Oregon.

Gerry C. Bower lived in Santa Ana, California, a few miles from Germain's. He thought he could improve the durability of the paper twist ties used for plant stakes by making a twist tie out of strips of PVC (polyvinyl chloride). He wanted a plant stake that was waterproof and resistant to sunlight. In 1952, he built a machine and a plant tie to do just that (U.S. Patent #2,767,113). He coated a wire with PVC and rolled it between two ribbons of PVC. He used a hot-air system to cure the adhesion.

In 1956, Bower invented a two-step method for making twist ties. He coated paper with polyethylene and cooled it. In the second step, he heated the wire and rolled it between two pieces of paper. His product (U.S. Patent # 3,068,135) may be considered the first modern twist tie.

In the late 1950s, Royal Industries, a conglomerate of small companies, purchased Gerry Bower's assets.[3] The new Royal Industries division took the name Plas-Ties and remained in Santa Ana.

Bakery

The evolution of the twist tie occurred on two new fronts following that in the agricultural industry. These were pushed by the development of polyethylene bags in the late 1950s, commonly used in the early 1960s.[4]

---

3. Some claim this was the company that made Royal Typewriters.
4. Low-density polyethylene was invented in 1942.

The story of bread in plastic bags begins with Otto Rohwedder, who invented the bread-slicing machine in 1928. He found only one bakery that would give his machine a chance, but it was an instant success with consumers. Their demand soon forced other bakeries to incorporate the bread slicer. Although consumers liked the innovation, sliced bread grew stale more quickly than unsliced bread. When sliced bread become more common in the early 1930s, bakeries wrapped it in wax paper and applied end labels to keep loaves fresher and slices together.

Wrapping loaves of bread was inefficient, and wax wrappers were not reclosable. To circumvent this problem, some bakers stuffed their bread into poly bags. The transition from wax paper to poly began as early as late 1960 or early 1961, but the bakery industry was resistant to the change and believed it a passing fad.

Bailey Smith, a past sales manager for Bedford Industries, once worked for Hefty (later acquired by Mobil), trying to sell poly bags to bakeries. He called bakeries for almost a full year before he made his first sale. Bakers initially turned down poly bags because they had already invested in automatic wax-paper-overwrap machines and did not want to put money into another technology. But one or two bakeries finally tried the poly bags tied with a twist tie. Because of its easy use and reclosability, consumers started to buy poly-bagged bread tied with a twist tie instead of the wax-paper-wrapped bread. To keep their market from competitors, bakeries adopted the new trend. Consumer demand forced poly bags, as well as sliced bread, onto the industry.

Though poly bags were more efficient than wrapping each loaf in wax paper, the bread had to be stuffed into the bag, the bag end twisted, and a cut twist tie applied—all steps by hand and requiring a lot of human labor on one bread line. The Rainbow Bakery in Oklahoma was looking to relieve some of the manual labor from this packaging process and heard that Earl Burford had developed the first automatic tying machine for farm machinery. The Rainbow Bakery asked Earl Burford whether he could make a tying machine for bread bags.[5] Earl told them, "Give me 30 days, and let me think about this."

At this time, twist ties were available only in cut lengths of just a few inches. Burford's farm machinery used a long roll of agriculture twine, cutting the material during the tying process. Earl Burford called Plas-Ties and asked whether it could make a continuous roll of twist tie. Plas-Ties said it could be done, solving Burford's first problem.

Earl Burford went back to his factory and built a machine to put twist ties on a bun bag. Thirty days later the machine was ready, and he took it to the bakery. Earl used poly bags loaded with hamburger buns to demonstrate the machine. The owner of Rainbow Bakery gave Burford his first order—for 19 machines. Earl went to his factory and started building more machines to fill the order. His first one shipped early in 1962.

The bread-bagging machine soon followed. A prototype was on display at the 1961 American Baking Association Convention and Exposition in Atlantic City.[6] Commodity Packaging Company of Yakima, Washington, developed the first commercially-available bagger—the Mark 50—in 1962. American Machine and Foundry Company (AMF, which made bowling equipment and once owned Harley-Davidson) purchased the patents to this machine around 1965.

---

5. Earl Burford is father of Charles Burford, now the sole owner of Burford Corporation.
6. Developed by Roy Willard and Bill Noyes, it was used at Buchan Bakery in Seattle in 1962.

Alvin C. Formo had been watching the poly-bagging industry since the 1961 convention. He believed it had great possibility, and he worked to develop his paddle bagger (similar to what bakeries use today) in 1964. That year, he founded Formost Packaging Machines Corporation in Seattle. Burford developed twist-tie machines for the AMF bagging lines and other lines for the Formost machines.

According to the Film and Bag Federation, the poly bag had taken 25 to 30 percent of the bread-packaging market by 1966. This growth encouraged about ten twist-tie companies across the country to enter the industry

Trash Bags

Two companies also formed on the East Coast, apart from the events to the west. One was Hanscom, which began manufacturing twist ties in 1953. Hanscom focused on the electrical cord market—hanking and bundling electrical cords with a twist tie.

The other early twist-tie company on the East Coast was Kimball,[7] which manufactured paper tags and labels, then strung them together with wire. The twist tie was a natural next step from its wired paper tags.

The growing trash-bag industry pushed the East Coast twist-tie companies. Harry Wasylyk of Winnipeg, Manitoba, and Larry Hansen of Lindsay, Ontario, Canada, invented the first polyethylene trash bag in 1950. This disposable, green trash bag intended for commercial use was originally sold to Winnipeg General Hospital. Hansen was working for the Union Carbide, which

---

7. Little is known about Kimball, but some believe the company was responsible for the start of many of the twist-tie companies on the East Coast.

eventually bought the invention from the two men and introduced the first consumer trash bag under the GLAD® trash-bag line in the mid-1960s.[8]

Before the introduction of the poly bag, consumers put garbage in paper sacks, such as grocery bags, and placed them in metal garbage cans. Poly bags allowed the trash to be consolidated into one, large bag. As trash rules became increasingly strict, trash-disposal services required that trash be sealed in poly bags.[9] The twist tie was the answer for easy sealing.

Seymour Glustein, president of Twist Tie Manufacturing in Montreal, Canada, watched the trash-bag industry develop in Canada. Glustein started working for Band Tie, a division of a large poly bag company in Montreal, in 1964. Band Tie had been importing twist ties from Plas-Ties but then built its own twist-tie line. Most of its customers were the produce and bakery departments of supermarkets.

After working at Band Tie for less than a year, Glustein knew the industry and thought he could do better on his own. Later in 1964, he formed his own company—Twist Tie Manufacturing—and went into direct competition with Band Tie. Struggling with internal problems, Band Tie failed a year later, leaving the Canadian twist-tie market to Glustein.

According to Glustein, until 1965, trash bags were unavailable to Canadian consumers—most did not even know what a trash bag was. But Union Carbide wanted to start a full-scale bag

---

8. The GLAD® brand originated with GLAD® Wrap in 1963. GLAD® Bags were launched between 1963 and 1965.
9. In 1969, for example, the New York City Sanitation Department conducted the "New York City Experiment" to show that poly bags used on curbside pickup were cleaner, safer, and quieter than metal trash-can pickup.

operation in the country. Its marketing plan was to distribute one GLAD® garbage bag to every household in Montreal. Union Carbide needed one twist tie to accompany each garbage bag and approached Glustein to make them. GLAD® had "a phenomenal campaign in Canada," its door-to-door distribution announced by posters and flyers throughout the city. "GLAD® just took off," and trash bags were soon the talk of the town.

In the United States, a few East Coast companies supplied twist ties for trash-bag manufacturers such as Union Carbide Corporation (GLAD®) and Mobil Chemical (Hefty). These companies provided gangs of twist ties (a sheet of twist ties cut to a certain length and perforated), which were hand-placed into boxes of trash bags.

One supplier was J. F. Auer. It had two machines to laminate paper to paper using a hotmelt system and operating in a 10,000-square-foot factory on the floor above A. L. A. Industries. A. L. A. Industries was owned by Phil Merlin, manufacturing electronics and fabricating Masonite® (used on the backs of TV sets to protect consumers from electrical shock).

J. F. Auer had been approached by Pollock, a wholesale paper company from Texas that sold plastic bakery bags, about putting its twist tie on a spool to sell with its poly bread bags. Auer struggled with spooling the tie. If each layer of twist tie was not perfectly laid, it caused snagging problems.

J. F. Auer asked Merlin to look at its spool-winding techniques because Merlin had done precision winding of cords for electronics. Merlin looked but did not wish to tackle the issue because of the spacing problems of twist tie and because he had other operations going. He was also concerned that bakeries, which operated 24 hours a day, might call him with problems in the middle of the night.

Merlin became interested in the twist-tie industry after Union Carbide Corporation approached J. F. Auer. Union Carbide had started extruding garbage bags and wanted a roll of gang ties on a spool—so the gangs could be cut to desired lengths for different products. Auer asked Merlin to help spool this project. "It would be like making toilet paper," Merlin thought. Auer gave him a machine to work with, and Merlin started manufacturing gang twist-ties in 1966—a division he soon named Alcar Industries.

From there, the twist-tie industry webbed. Associated Plastics and Alcar Industries led the way to twist ties for trash bags on the East Coast. Alcar birthed T and T Industries, Inc. Leading in the bread-bag industry were Plas-Ties, Package Containers, DuPont (who invented the plastic/plastic twist tie in 1964), and newcomers St. Regis Paper (which previously bought ties), Tite Ties, and Bedford Industries. Germain's stayed largely in the agricultural sector, from which Plas-Ties was beginning to move.

The twist tie evolved independently on three fronts. Phil Merlin, for instance, said he was unaware of the twist-tie market on the West Coast until 1969. There were about 12 companies manufacturing twist tie in 1970—the industry's peak. Manufacturers Burford, Plas-Ties, Clements Industries, Inc., and Doboy were developing twist-tie application machinery to make packaging more efficient. And the industry was expanding internationally as Plas-Ties licensed its process to companies in Japan, Denmark, and Canada.

The Twist Tie of the Future

The next 30 years brought many changes, and the original twist-tie companies in North America dropped to five by 2004. A few closed their doors, but many merged with other companies in a series of acquisitions during the mid-1970s and early 1980s. It was a common economic occurrence—when customers consolidate and become fewer, suppliers must consolidate as well. Bakeries founded and owned by single families were bought by one of several national bakery chains. The same thing happened with the paper companies that had distributed cut twist ties to trash-bag manufacturers. As customers decreased in number and increased in size, the suppliers were forced to do the same.

After its founding in 1966, Bedford Industries moved into a leadership position, making many important industry innovations, including the plastic/paper tie, with wire adhering to the tie so that it did not protrude from the end, and the all-plastic (plastic/plastic) tie.

Twist-tie uses and markets have continued to evolve. The product has entered some markets that probably were not considered by its inventors—the medical field and technological packaging, for instance. Bedford Industries has moved the twist tie into these advanced industries, where the twist tie is a common component of face masks and surgical drapes as well as of RFID (radio-frequency identification) technology.

Today's twist tie follows in the footsteps of its predecessors. Just as the first agricultural twist tie leapt to bread and trash bags, the twist tie of today leaps from bakery to surgical room. Keep an eye on this little-noticed item. Who knows what it might do next?

Bedford Bets Big on SPPF*

Bedford is best known for wire ties. But it backs its belief in new PP-container forming process with $2.5 million. Now it's ready to roll.

On the surface, it would appear that Bedford Industries, Inc., Worthington, Minn., is shifting its packaging gears. Best known as a major producer of wire ties for packaging and for consumer products, Bedford has invested $2.5 million to become the most integrated commercial source for oriented polypropylene containers produced by solid-phase pressure forming (SPPF).

That's quite a claim, but the best available information seems to reinforce it. Here's why:

• After three years of assessment and evaluation, Bedford took delivery a year ago of a Gabler FP700 thermoformer specially designed for the SPPF process developed in the US by Shell Chemical. The company has been experimenting and testing this machine, which has an output of over 150 containers/min from one of Bedford's 10-up container tools. A second FP700 is now en route from the Gabler factory in Lubeck, West Germany.

• Later in '81, Bedford received its first two smaller Gabler Tima D450 thermoformers that it is now using to produce

---

*   This article originally appeared in the June 1982 issue of *Packaging Digest*, which has graciously granted permission for its inclusion in this volume.

173

lids and overcaps via the SPPF process. Each machine has a capacity of about 100/min. Four more of these machines will be added in the coming months, with production space left to bring its total to eight.

- Early this year, an extrusion line for PP was installed. The Welex 4.5-in. extruder has an output of about 1,500 lb/hr. That will be sufficient, says Bob Ludlow, Bedford president, to supply its two FP700 formers and eight of the smaller Tima D450s.

- Just last month, Bedford began installation of the first of two Van Dam offset printers. Both will initially be set up for up to four-color printing, although each is capable of taking two additional print stations. One, a 560L, will handle bowls and cups at speeds to 225/min. The second, a Model 460SL, has a capacity of up to 275 lids/min.

- All of this equipment is housed in a spacious new plant addition, designed with climate and air-pressure controls. Provisions were made to keep this high-technology addition as free of contamination as possible.

What makes Bedford's operation unique among other early U.S. entries in this technology is its extrusion/forming/decorating capabilities for both containers and lids or caps. This puts the company in the forefront of one of the most interesting new processes in plastics containers.

Why SPPF?

Certainly this is a question being asked by a number of injection molders, perhaps by some packagers too. Solid-phase pressure forming, at its most basic, is a technology that permits high-speed containers to be made from specially formulated polypropylene resins. PP has limitations that restrict its use in most conventional manufacturing processes.

Particularly at the time that Shell Chemical developed this process, PP had been an economical alternative to injection molding and other thermoforming resins. But economy aside, the material's characteristics make it ideal for food packaging. Its combination of properties include: moisture barrier and chemical resistance, cleanliness and stress-crack resistance. Its transparency is superior to some other resins. It has good toughness and stiffness. It can be sterilized or hot-glued and is receptive to printing. However, its low melt strength and narrow temperature range had rendered it impractical in molding and forming.

Shell discovered that PP could be formed at temperatures just below its melt point, while still in the solid state or phase. This led to the further development of processing techniques that incorporate plug-assist and high pressure in the forming operation. Bedford Industries and a handful of other U.S. firms are now licensed by Shell to use the process. The U.S. pioneer, Ardmore Farms, Deland, Fla., is committed to captive container-making for its juices.

The July issue of *Packaging Digest* will sketch a broader picture of the companies that use SPPF for packaging.

Bedford's Rationale

While the mix of SPPF and wire ties would seem unusual, Bedford has been extruding plastics for 16 years (mostly high-density polyethylene). It has done a modest amount of thermoforming for six years. Bedford began evaluating SPPF four years ago, before its U.S. debut. Several visits to European pressure forming operations convinced Bob Ludlow of the potential; he recognized the importance of the precision involved.

"There's really no magic in solid-phase pressure forming. But it does require extremely precise attention to materials, tooling and process controls. More so than most processes we're familiar with here," he says. Ludlow felt his firm could establish the same "proprietary" approach that it employs towards its closely guarded wire-tie manufacturing

Already the company has moved into making its own prototype tooling in-house. This cuts to 30 days the time needed to go from an approved container design to finished samples for further testing. For the foreseeable future, Ludlow says that production tooling will probably continue to be made overseas. Eventually, he hopes that demand will prompt U.S. mold makers to develop the technology to produce them here.

When Bedford committed to its first FP700 from Gabler, its market evaluation indicated that SPPF had great potential for margarine tubs. At that time, Ludlow says, existing bowls were either a heavy 16-g injection-molded PE or thermoformed from expensive methacrylate-butadiene-styrene (MBS). "Against those materials, our resin costs for a bowl with similar performance characteristics would be a third cheaper. Since then, many molders have cut down the weight by going to thinwall molding. That's narrowed our advantage somewhat. However, if we go thinwall, we can take the container weights down too."

There appear to be some inherent advantages with PP and the SPPF process. In the main, SPPF can allow packagers to use a lighter-weight container without sacrificing strength, sometimes significantly lighter.

A container made by SPPF is oriented, much like a blow-molded plastic beverage bottle. Bedford claims that it can produce a 403-finish margarine bowl at weights of either 9.2 or

8.2 g with characteristics that are competitive with a 12-g standard injection-molded version and better than a 9.5-g thinwall molded tub. Depending on a packager's needs, says Bedford, the SPPF process can take this container down to as little as 5.2 g for maximum resin savings.

Material Controls Costs

The greatest benefit of SPPF for packagers is that it's a two-step operation offering great flexibility. Injection-molding systems require changes in tooling and/or extrusion programming to vary the weights of the finished parts. With SPPF, the molding process remains the same; the only change is in the sheetstock that's fed into the thermoformer.

For the 403 margarine cups, Bedford says it can produce weights from 9.2 g down to 5.2 g all in a single afternoon! That's done by simply changing the 45-mil sheet down to 25 mil at 5-mil increments. Then, following a cure of about 24 hrs, the various samples can be run through full tests.

This sounds easy, and in theory it is. But as Bedford's experience attests, it involves a substantial amount of skill and precision, not only for the thermoformer but in its extrusion line as well. Bad cups can come from good material, but it's absolutely impossible to make good cups from poor material, Ludlow states firmly. That's one of the primary reasons Bedford added the Welex extrusion line in January. Since then, it has piggybacked its previous extrusion experience with the PP-extrusion recommendations from Frank Nissel of Welex and others.

It has been running both homopolymer PP and a copolymer version as well, from resin supplied by both Shell and Hercules. The homopolymer is less expensive and produces containers with more stiffness than the copolymer. But for low-temperature performance and stress-crack resistance, the copolymer PP is the favored material.

The 4.5-in. extruder was selected for its output, 1,500 lb/hr. That, Ludlow says, is sufficient to match the production needs of Bedford's thermoforming volume from two FP700 bowl machines and eight D450 lid formers. After slitters cut the material to the appropriate web width, the scrap is automatically led directly into a Cumberland grinder. Regrind is fed back to the virgin resin hopper. Ludlow says it's been successful with materials containing as much as 50 percent of regrind.

Based on its experience, Bedford's main concern with extrusion is to avoid stressing the PP sheet. This will result in problems when the material is formed.

"You need to have consistent sheet going into the thermoformer," Ludlow says, "because you can't be adjusting the machine conditions all the time. There's no way you can get solid output when you're trying to react to changes in the material. All the tolerances are too tight."

Sheet stressed in extrusion will react differently when preheated in the thermoformer. It exhibits some pull and twist as it moves through the heating banks, and the stress is relieved by the heat. The result is poor consistency in formed containers.

To avoid the stress requires a delicate balance of all the variables in the extrusion. Pulling the sheet too fast may stretch it. Or nipping the extrusion head down too much can cause problems. There are other variables and all need to be properly balanced. Bedford's quality control has become very tight.

Lab Sophistication

Throughout the project Bedford has recognized the need to consult with specialists. It retained consultants in Europe, both to gain entry into plants doing pressure forming there and later to gain ideas from extrusion operations.

For in-house QC, it outfitted Tom Haddock, a polymer chemist, with a plastics technical laboratory for testing resin, sheet and finished containers. For its ongoing machinery maintenance and installation, Bedford retains the services of Peter Gielisse, a European-trained consultant with a Ph.D. in mechanical engineering. Combined with Bedford's engineering staff, this gives the company the impressive support a highly technical process like SPPF requires—particularly when it takes place in southwestern Minnesota.

And a German-speaking production supervisor helps too. He works directly with Gabler engineers from Germany. This was a planned relationship. Machine considerations aside, "we felt it would be an advantage to work direct with the machinery builders instead of US representatives," Ludlow states. "The technical support has been excellent."

Gabler was attractive to the Bedford president because of its size. It's a major German engineering company, although thermoforming equipment was a relatively minor factor. "They have had several years' experience with pressure forming in Europe, and we knew how badly they wanted their first U.S. installation to be successful," Ludlow shrewdly observes. Before opting for Gabler, Bedford had narrowed the contenders to those using in-mold trimming.

It was the combination of in-mold trim and the stacker/loader system that tilted the scales toward Gabler equipment.

Machine Features

"We don't believe that any system with separate molding and trimming operations can offer the consistency and uniformity that you get with in-mold trimming," Ludlow says "Plus downstream trimming introduces a separate function that needs to be controlled very carefully. Once the sheet is captured in the molding step, the trimming can be done to very tight tolerances.

In the operation, the roll sheetstock is unwound and fed into the heat tunnel. It consists of infrared ceramic-medium heaters, mounted top and bottom. The heater assembly is track-mounted. It can be easily rolled away from the machine bed for threading of a sheet web, then rolled back into position. The preheat system involves five separate, controllable zones to uniformly bring the PP to 320 deg F as it's indexed over the female forming dies.

At this point, the top die with plug assist descends and clamps tight around each of the cavities. In the 403 container size, Bedford's tooling has a 2x5 cavity arrangement. It produces 10 containers/cycle from a 28.5-in. web. As the plug assist forces the preheated material into the water-jacket-cooled dies, 100-psi air pressure is released through the plug to spread the material before the platen releases, the cutting mechanism descends just a fraction of an inch to cleanly separate each part from the web.

Cups and web move forward a short distance. Then an overhead vacuum belt picks up the cups while the scrap web is forced down to the rewind roller below the machine. The vacuum belt carries the cups to the automatic stacker/loader mechanism. Guide rails keep each row separate as the cups move forward and down a waterfall-style chute. Reciprocating arms at the bottom of each channel then move each individual cup to nest over the previous cups. This extended collating area can hold several minutes of production, while one worker sets up the lined shipping cases. Nested stacks of cups are inserted into bags before being loaded into cases. A worker can comfortably handle transfer of cups from machine to case.

This efficient and space-saving discharge system was also a strong advantage to the Gabler system, Ludlow says. The company also liked the cam drive of the forming station, along with toggle drives on the overhead platen for high locking pressure. The system has the capability of more than 15 cycles/min; Bedford's operating range now is 13 to 14 cycles.

The Tima D450 lid formers are essentially scaled-down versions of the process. However, in place of the elaborate loading/stacking system, the Timas simply eject the lids upward into a vertical magazine for bagging and packoff.

Decorating Off-line

Bedford has found that SPPF pieces require a 24-hr cure time for best results. So its decorating or printing systems will be separate from forming. As mentioned earlier, its Van Dam 560L for cup or bowl sidewalls was just being installed at the time of PD's visit; the Van Dam 460SL will be installed soon.

"We selected these machines because of their versatility and quality. Potential customers told us they wanted 'Van Dam-quality' printing, and we felt they are the best available machines for our use," Ludlow says. Each will initially have four print stations. Two more could be added later.

Another factor, one that Bob Ludlow feels will become important down the road, is that these machines can be modified to handle square containers. This is the most popular shape for margarine products in most of Europe, he reports. The U.S. market might shift that way in the future. The Van Dam printers routinely handle the square shapes overseas. Different mandrels are required, and speeds are somewhat less than the 225 containers/min Bedford expects with rounds.

The Gabler equipment also has experience in forming squared containers. Tooling for this shape is an accomplished craft in Europe. Near-term, though, Bedford plans to move into delicatessen containers. Tooling is now being completed using mold inserts that will allow use of the same dies for different cup capacities.

Together with Ted Ludlow, vice president of sales and marketing, Bob is now beginning to talk seriously to potential users. "We had been holding back until we were really confident that we were ready for production runs. Now we have to let packagers know what our capabilities are. After all, not many know that we do anything but make wire ties."

Injection molders anticipated the availability of PP containers produced by SPPF, the Ludlows discovered.

"There already is considerable work being done to cut weights by moving to thinwall molding. We feel that pressure-formed OPP containers and lids can demonstrate better characteristics with lighter weights. Plus, we can run samples on our production equipment at a variety of weights in a single afternoon," Bob Ludlow says confidently.

"We think our investment in this process puts us in a unique position to offer containers and lids, either or both fully decorated. And I'm convinced that we have the best chance to duplicate the lightweight European containers, either round or square."

Covering Its Capping Bet

Snap-on overcaps or lids of OPP, produced by the SPPF process, differ in skirt configuration from the standard injection-molded caps of PE. The thermoforming process for OPP does not permit the undercut design that injection molders use to lock onto a container's top bead.

The result is that thermoformed caps or lids cannot be automatically applied with the equipment used for injection-molded versions. Despite this handicap, Bedford feels there is a definite market for economical OPP lids and overcaps. Often using a 15-mil sheetstock, pressure-formed lids have a significant potential for resin savings, Bob Ludlow says.

Recognizing the problems with application, Bedford purchased automatic overcapping equipment from three leading manufacturers—Donahower, McKenna, and Holmatic. It then provided each manufacturer with development funds to engineer their systems to handle thermoformed closures.

"Thermoformed lids roll differently from injection-molded ones," Ludlow says. "Each manufacturer modified his machine for the thermoformed caps. The changes are primarily in cap handling and feeding. We use the machines for our own testing.

"Our studies show that there is enough economy in converting from injection-molded to thermoformed lids to offer payback on a completely new machine within a year."

Ludlow reports that thermoformed lids did suffer one setback. A major whipped-topping manufacturer had converted to thermoformed lids, then went back to the injection-molded style. However, Ludlow says, the packager's problems were related to uniformity. Its thermoforms had been produced on a system that forms in one position but cuts downstream. In-mold trimming, he says, will virtually assure consistency.

With thinner lids, along with cups or bowls, Ludlow believes the decision of how much to lighten weight may be determined by the importance a packager places on consumer reuse of the container.

Sources

Printed Sources

"Bedford Bets Big on SPPF." *Packaging Digest,* June 1982: 64–66 (see pages 173–83 of this volume for complete story).

"Bedford Bonds Are Approved by City Council." *Worthington Daily Globe,* January 25, 1973.

"Bedford Celebrates 20 Years." *Worthington Daily Globe,* September 1986 (undated clipping).

"Bedford Workers Get Lavish Praise." *Worthington Daily Globe,* May 23, 1974.

"Bend Over Backwards." *Creative Products News,* August 1990.

Birmingham, Fredrich. *Ball Corporation: The First Century.* Indianapolis: Curtis, 1980.

Brandenburg, Jim. "Two New Local Industries to Hold Open House." *Worthington Daily Globe,* May 1974 (undated clipping).

Callison, Jill. "Bedford Markets Ribbon." *Worthington Daily Globe,* September 16, 1990.

———. "Bedford Molding Success from Plastics." *Worthington Daily Globe,* September 20, 1986.

Cashel, Robert. "Bedford to Expand in S.D." *Worthington Daily Globe,* April 3, 1984.

———. "Ludlow to Build New Plant Here." *Worthington Daily Globe,* October 12, 1972.

Dayton, Bruce B., and Ellen B. Green. *George Draper Dayton: A Man of Parts.* Minneapolis: Privately published, 1997.

Hawley, David. "Bedford Is 'Tying up World.'" *Worthington Daily Globe,* May 23, 1974.

"Increases Production Efficiency While Holding Costs in Line" (editorial). *Baking Industry,* July 1976: 22.

LaFlame, James. "Switch to Paper/Plastic Ties for Bread Bags Reduces Costs at Florida Bakery." *Baking Industry,* April 1978.

"Ludlow Credits Town Support for Success." *Worthington Daily Globe,* May 23, 1974.

Ludlow, Pamela Byron. "Ludlow Family History" (family manuscript), 1994.

Ludlow, Peter. *Semantics, Tense and Time.* Cambridge, Massachusetts: MIT Press, 1999.

Ludlow, Robert. "Promoting Ethical Business Practices." *Small Business Report,* June 1987.

Novak, Jay. "Bedford Industries: A Simple Product, Efficient Energy Use." *Worthington Daily Globe,* July 12, 1979.

"A 'Slice' of History: Inventor's Son Returns to Where Sliced Bread Began." (Chillicothe, Missouri) *Constitution-Tribune,* August 2003 (undated clipping).

Swanson, William. "More Than Family Ties." *Minnesota Technology* Winter 1993: 7–9.

"The Ties That Bind." *Packaging Pictorial,* Spring 1974: 11–14.

"Tiny Tools That Have a Million Uses." *Reflections* 1 (1999): 9–12.

"Twist-Ties Mark Trail." (Little Rock) *Arkansas Democrat Gazette,* August 4, 1988.

Personal Interviews by the Author

Boushek, Robert, August 15, 2002.

Cook, Norma, July 2002.

Fisher, Keith (group, recorded), May 2003.

Glustein, Seymour (phone), July 20, 2004.

Haddock, Thomas, June 24 and 28 and July and August 2002; June 23, 25, and 26, 2003.

Hanson, Mary (group, recorded), May 2003.

Hill, Robert (phone), June 27 and July 21, 2003.

Holmes, Dale (group, recorded), May 2003.

Ivey, Donald (phone), June 21, 2004.

Jenkins, Garold, July 2002.

Langland, Terry (group, recorded), May 2003.

Lauro, Bob (phone), June 2003.

Linquist, John, June 2003.

Ludlow, Patricia, July 22, 2003.

Ludlow, Robert, June, July, and August 2002; June 2003; and June 21, 2004.

Ludlow, Ted (phone), June 24, 2003.

Merlin, Philip (phone), June 21, 2004.

Milbrandt, Kim, July 2002.

Milbrandt, Sarah Ludlow, July 2002.

Moore, Doyle, June 28, 2002.

Patrick, William D. (phone), June 23, 2004.

Radloff, Beth, July 21, 2003.

Story, Gene (phone), June 26, 2004.

Taylor, John, July 9, 2002.

Tinklenberg, Lloyd, July 2002.

Tschetter, Jeff, July 24, 2003.

Van Ede, John, July 2002 and (group, recorded) May 2003.

Whiting, Robert R. (phone), June 24, 2004.

Index

Page numbers in italics indicate topic illustrations.

120; deli market, 78, 81; East Coast market, 80, 137; fast-food industry, 63; floral industry, 109, 111–13, 116, 118, 120–21, 147; garbage/trash-bag industry, 79, 103, 141, 149, 168; grocery/supermarket industry, 141–44, 150, 181; market expansion, 66; home, shop, and garden market, 79; medical industry, 63, 136, 146, 149–50, 172; packaging industry, 52, 172; paper industry, 172; produce industry, 142–43, 147, 150; retail industry, 147; visual display industry, 113, 119

products: annual production, 61; banners/ribbons, 118; bendable ribbon, 110–17; bundler (Ring Tier), 126; containers (plastic, paper), 63–64, 69, 76, 83–84, 87–89, 181, *77*; craft kits, 112–13; cup lids, 63; decorative/custom ties, 109–10; design (custom/printing), 115; double-wired ribbon, 116; double-wire twist tie, 48, 103, 121; exercise wheel, *52*–53; gang-tie, *42*–43, 103; half-inch twist tie, 143; lids/overcaps, 183; Limblight trail markers, 102; lumber (plastic/recycled), 104–08, 120, 130; margarine containers, 181; medical face masks, 136; medical surgical drapes, 136; Microlite® bowls, 83–85; micro-wavable bowls, trays, and packages, 82–85, *88*, 149; plastic spools, 53; ovenable bowls/trays, *88*; "ovenable" twist tie, 43; packaging machines, 126; paper core, 53–54; plastic/paper tie, 49, 56–57; precision-wound tie, 53–*54*, 55; roofing (Rolath®), 107; skip adhesive, *see* Peel &

Stick®; specialized ties, 102; spool adapter (spoolless-tie system), 53–*54*, 55–*57*, 58; trays (candy/cookie/TV-dinner), 71–*72*, 87; Twist 'N Tie brand name, 79; twist tie, 3, 12, 15, 21, 66, 102, 116, 149, 153; twist-tie applicator machines, 123–*24*, 125–*26*

R & J Wholesale Supply, Sioux Falls, SD, 110
R Line, machinery, 146
radio frequency identification (RFID), 147, 172
Radloff, Beth, 187
raffia, 163, 164
Rainbow Bakery, OK, 166–67
Rampart, *see* Shell Corp.
Raven Industries, Inc., Sioux Falls, SD, 13–14, 31
recycled plastic, *see* products, lumber; products, roofing
Reker, Dave, 135
Ring Tier, *see* products, bundler
Rohwedder, Dick, 28–29, 38, 41, 55, 101
Rohwedder, Otto, 28, 166
Rolath®, *see* products, roofing
Royal Industries, *see* Plas-Ties Corp.
Rushmore State Bank, *see* First National Bank of Rushmore

St. Regis Paper Co., 71, 133–34, 159, 171
Saran™, 64
Schapp's Salvage, Worthington, 104
Sheldahl, Inc., Northfield, MN, 48
Shell Chemical, 173, 175, 177
Shell Corp., Rampart division, 88
Schindler, Walter R., 164
Small Business Report, articles, 93–94
Smith, Bailey, 166
Snap-A-Tag®, *142*, 146

Twenty-two-year-old Jay Milbrandt is the grandson of Bob and Pat Ludlow. As an undergraduate he worked summers at Bedford Industries as a graphic artist intern and research analyst. Recently graduated from Bethel University in St. Paul, Minnesota, with a double-major in philosophy and international business, he now attends the School of Law and Graziadio School of Business at Pepperdine University in Malibu, California. He expects to complete his jurist doctorate and master's degree in business administration (JD/MBA) in the spring of 2008.

The main text of this book is set in 12-point Bodoni ITC-TT Book; other type blocks are variations of that face. The text stock is Mohawk 80# Bright White Matte Text. The endsheets are Passport 80# Sandstone Felt. The cloth edition is Smyth-sewn and bound in Arrestox B Linen-Set Hickory and Vanilla with blind and gold-foil stamps.

Editing/design: Ellen Green, E. B. Green Editorial, St. Paul
Indexing: Patricia Green, Homer, Alaska
Printing: Sexton Printing, Inc., St. Paul
Binding: Midwest Editions, Minneapolis